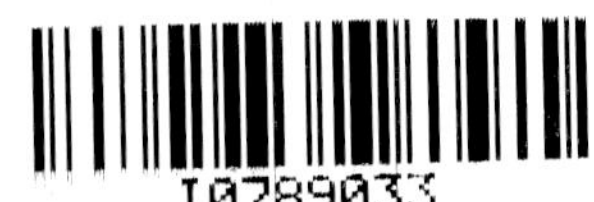

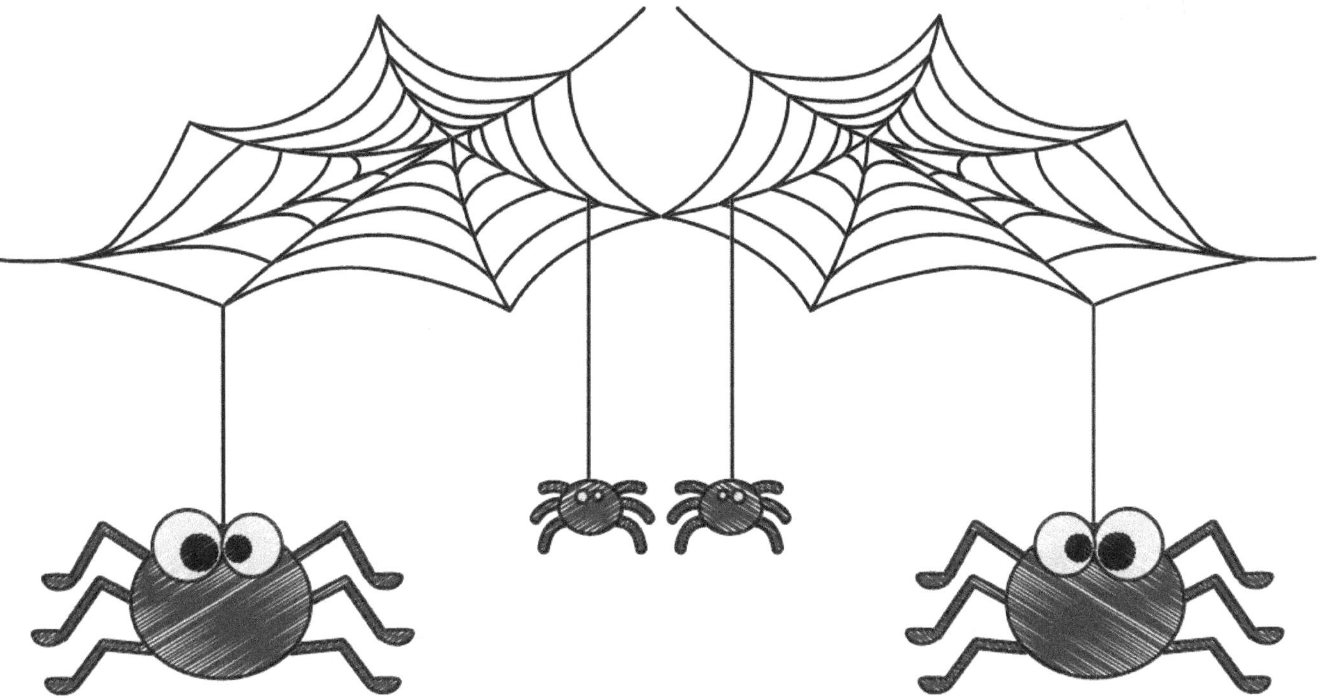

This book belongs to

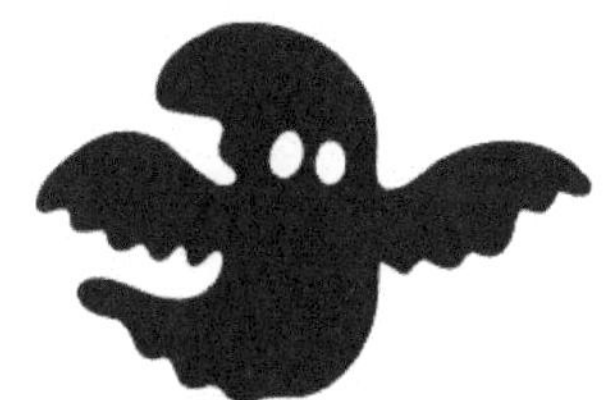
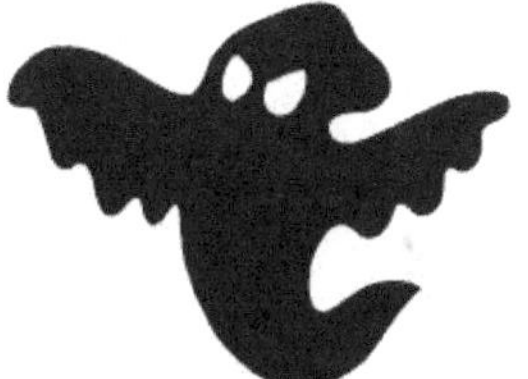

____

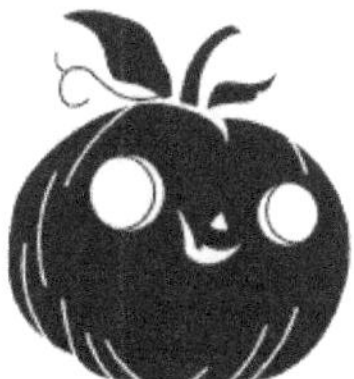
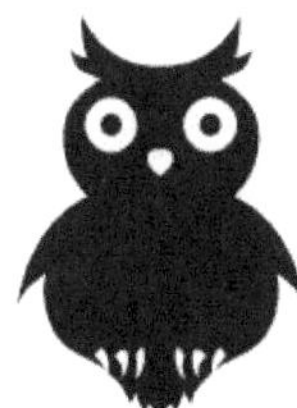
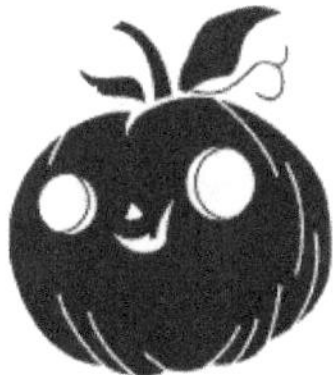

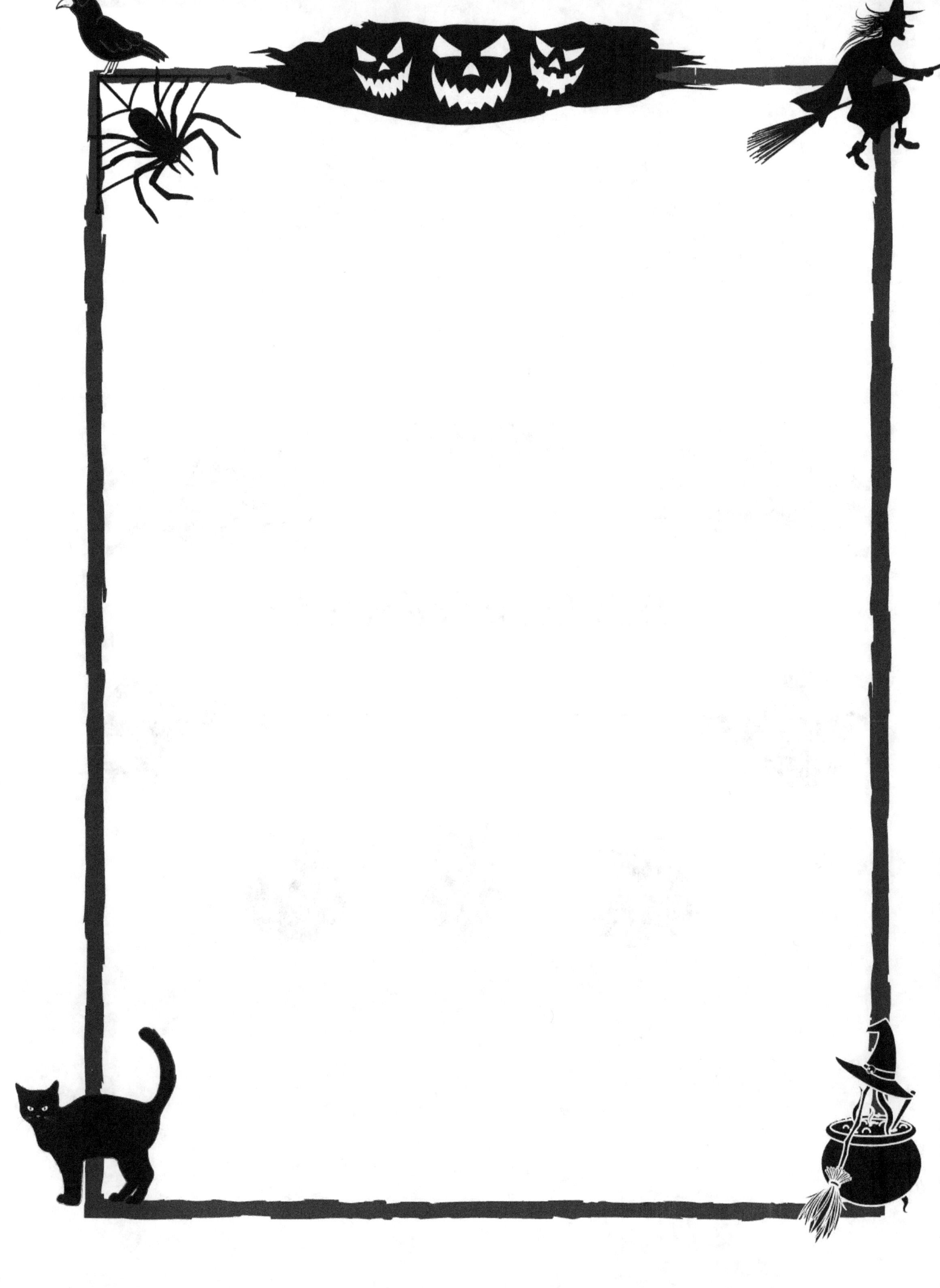

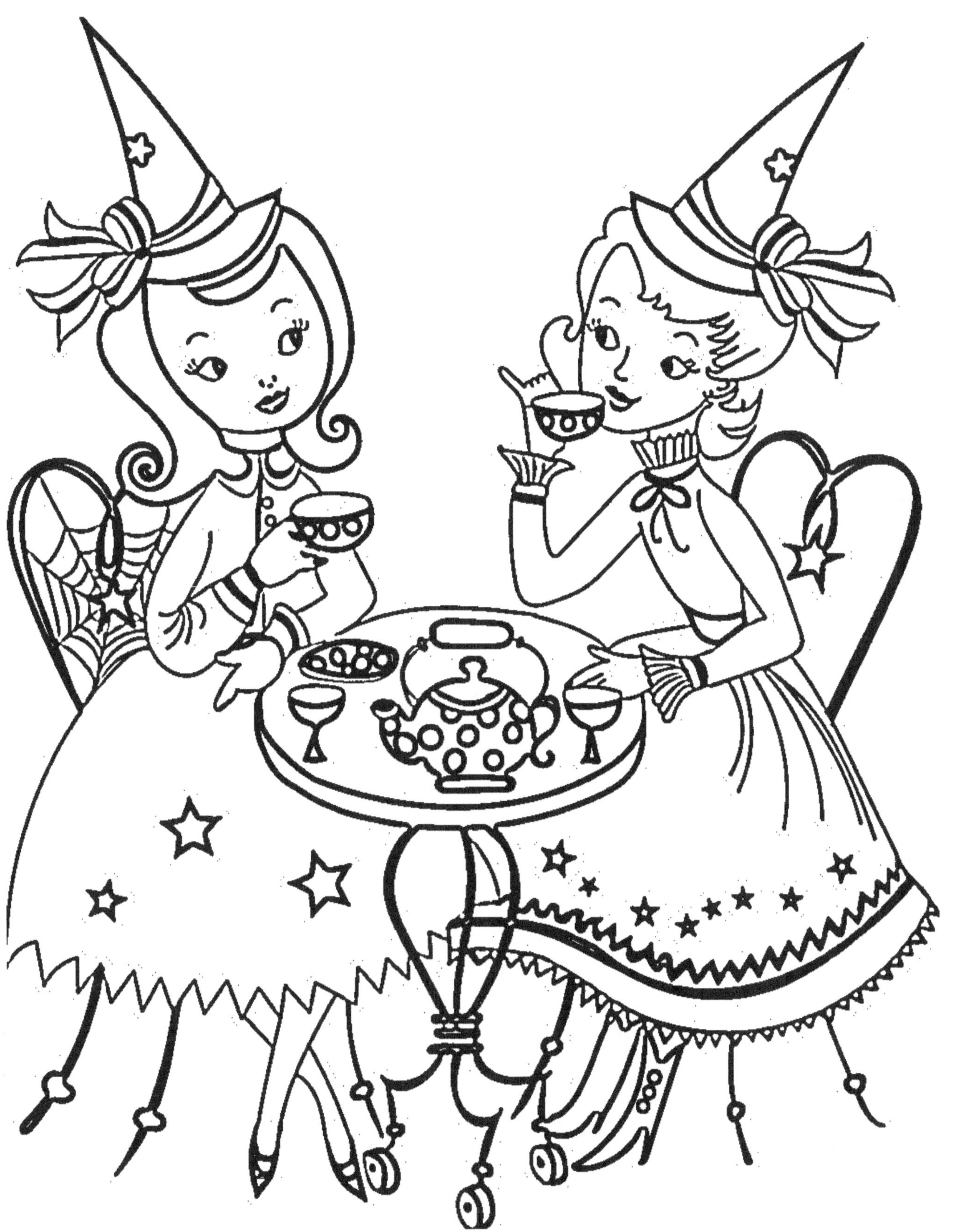

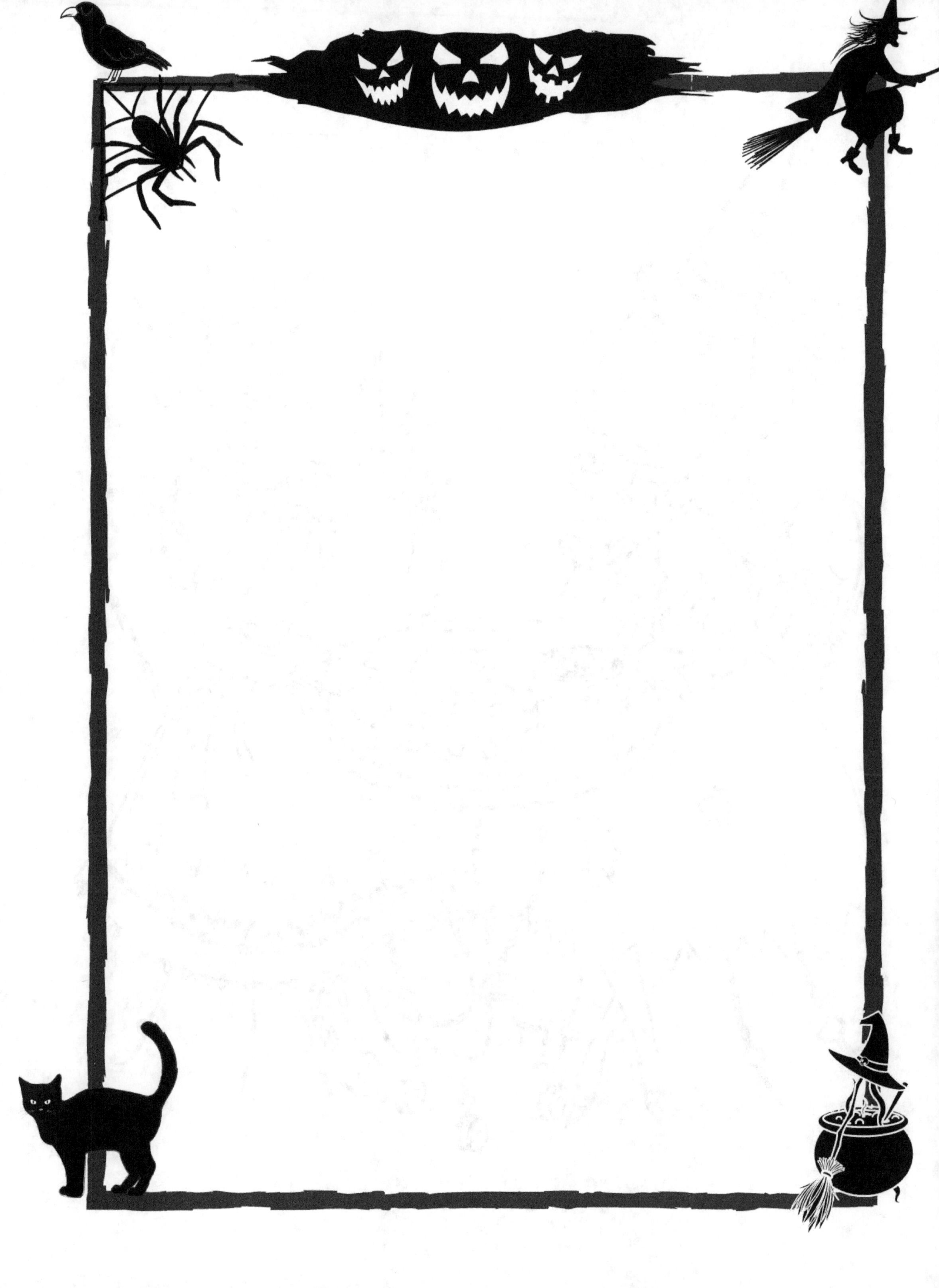

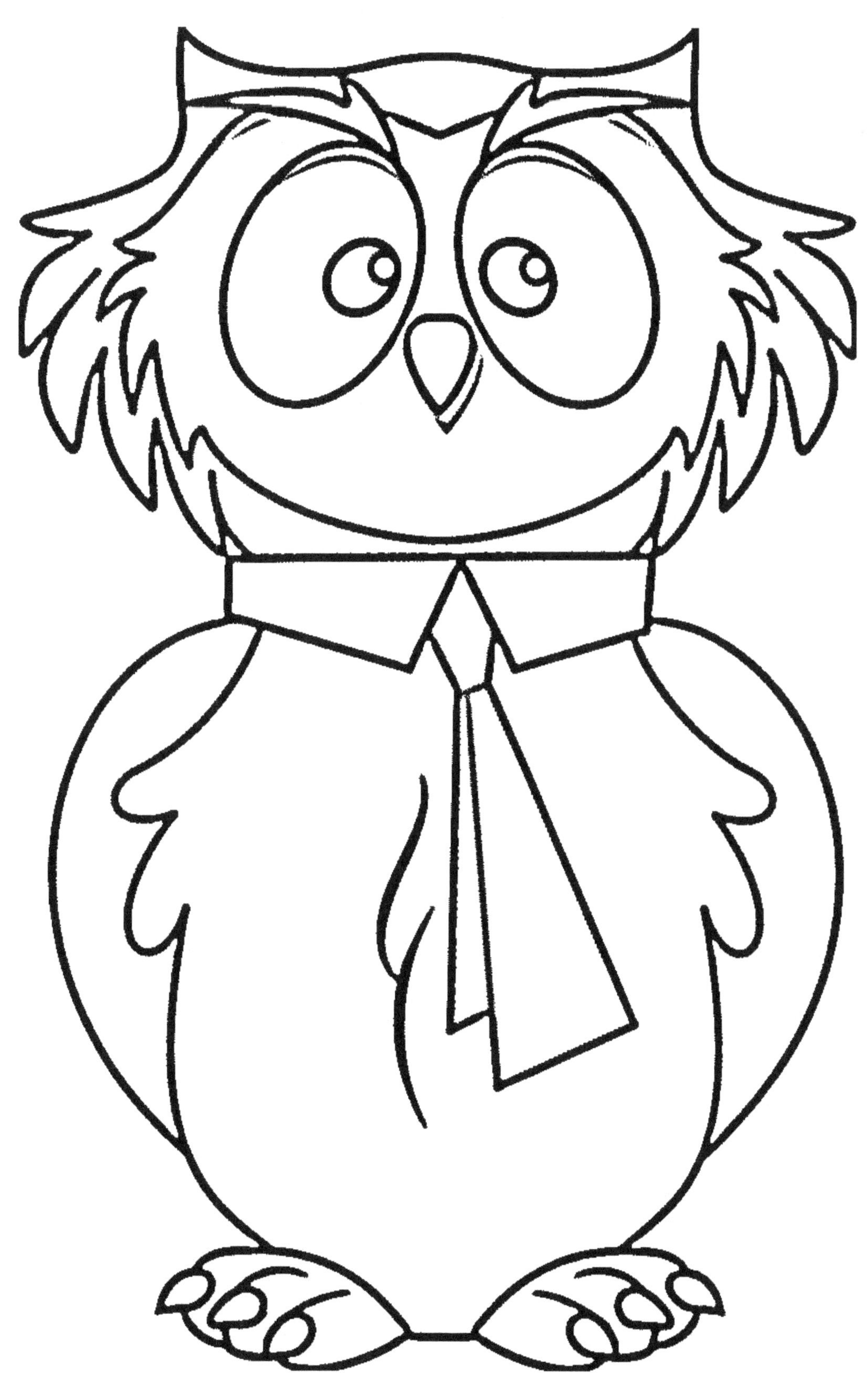

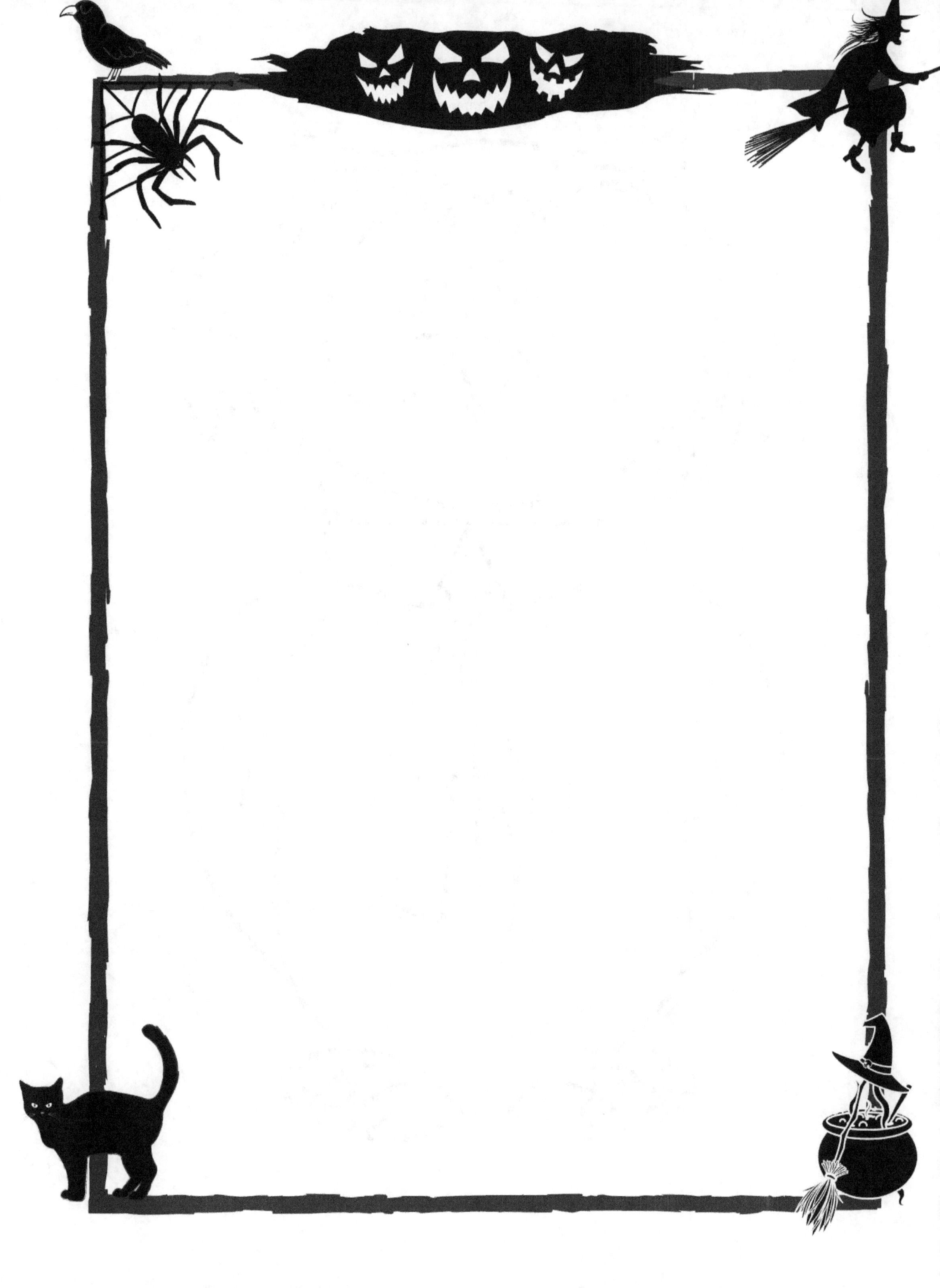

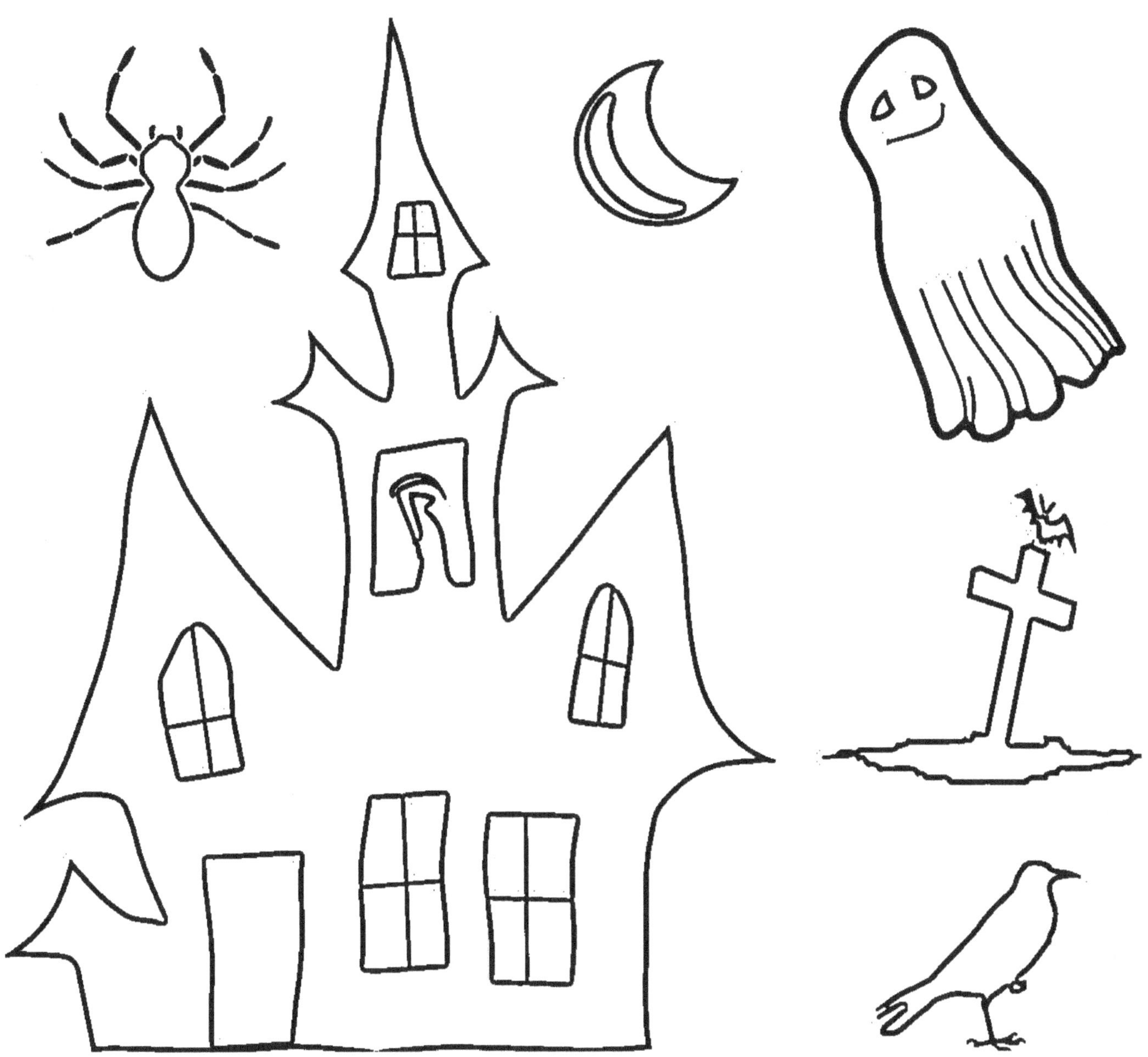

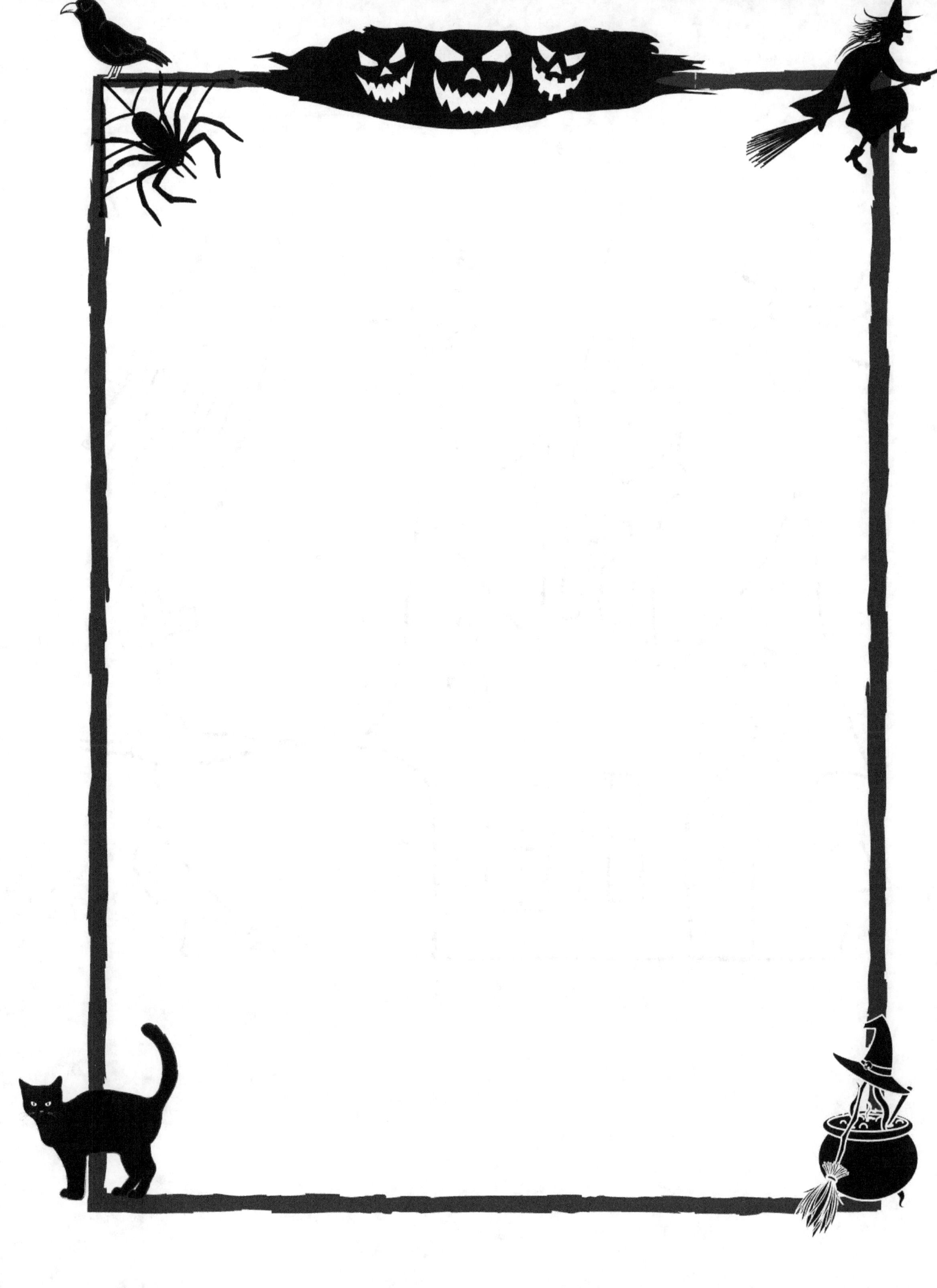

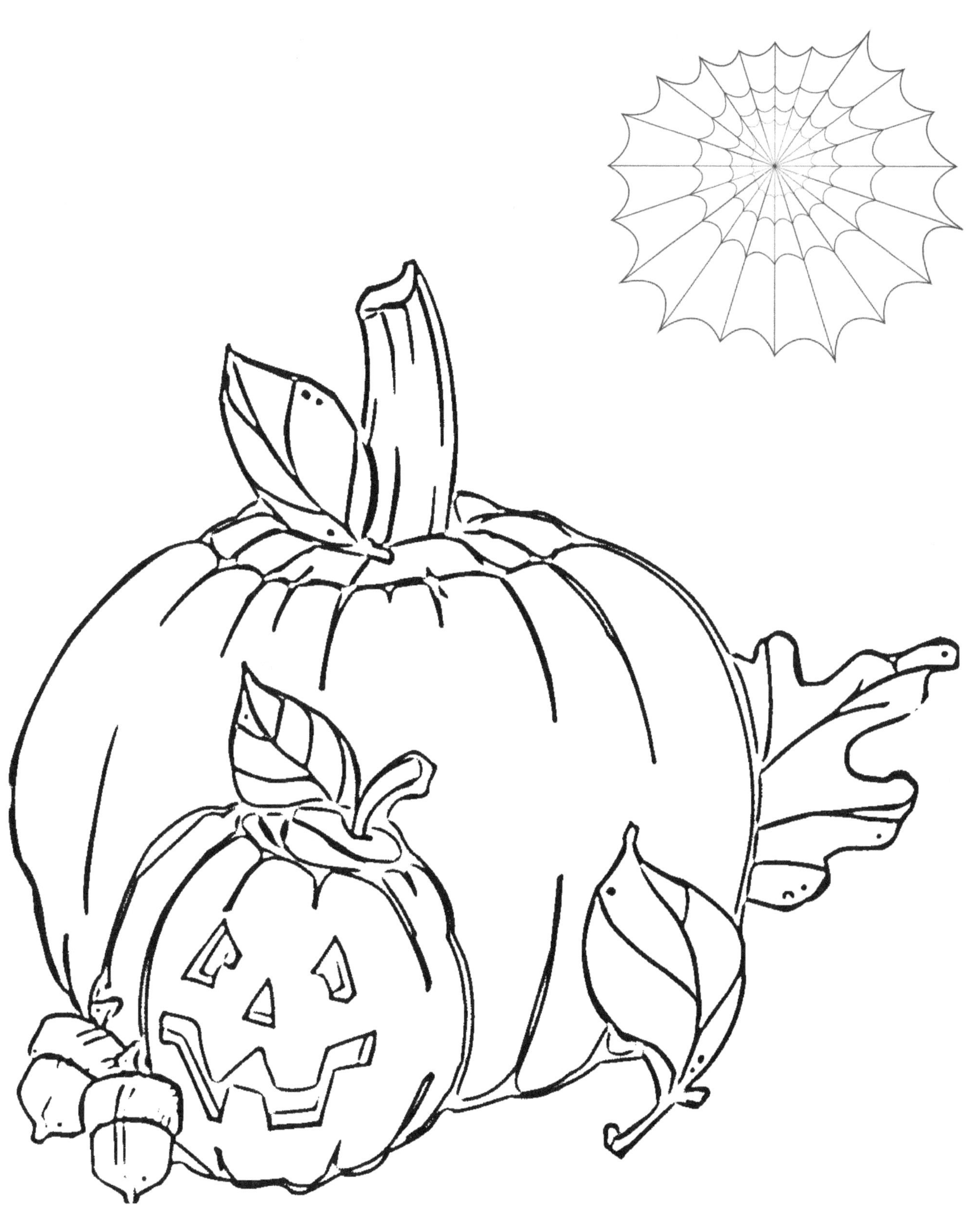

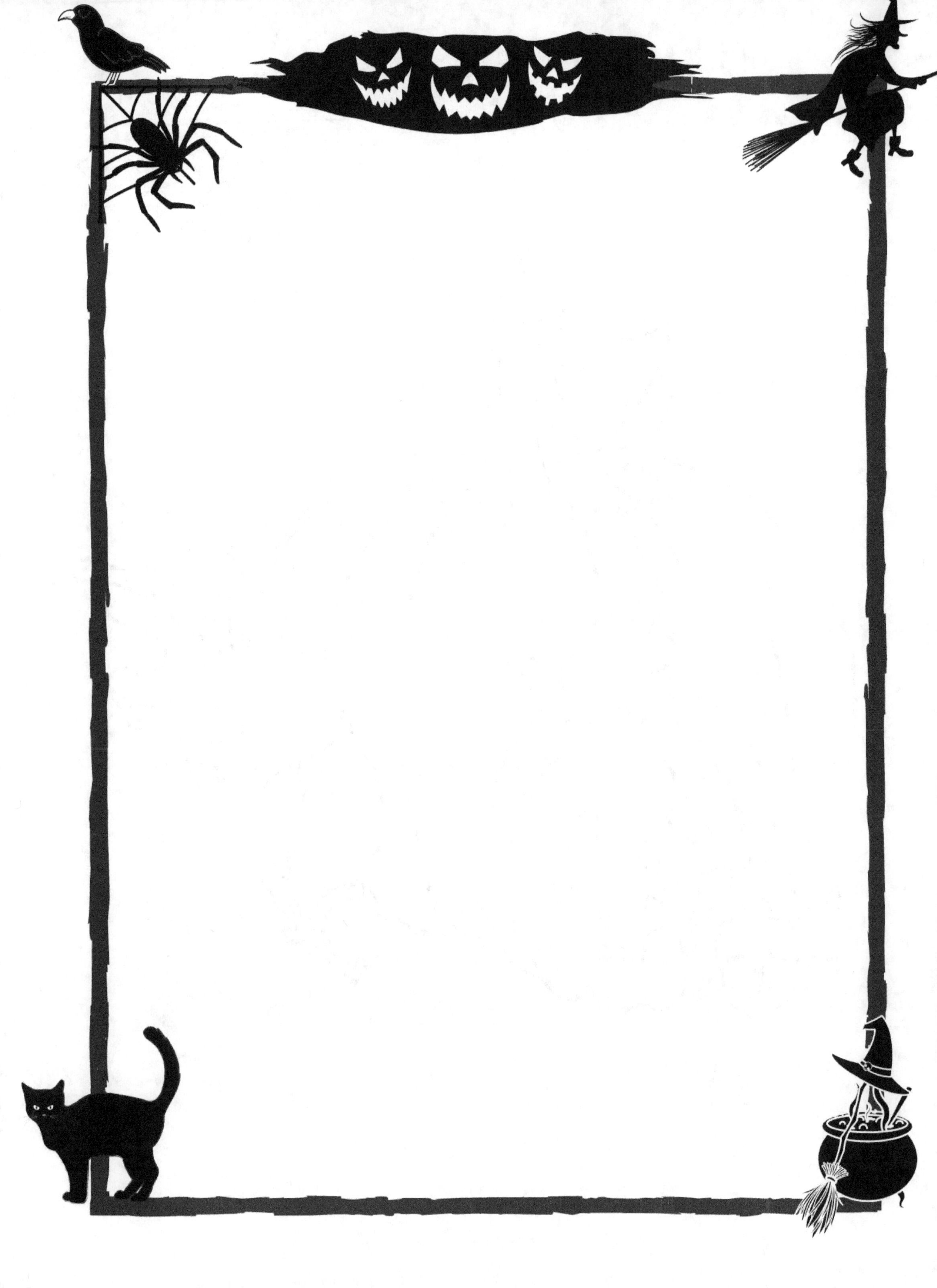

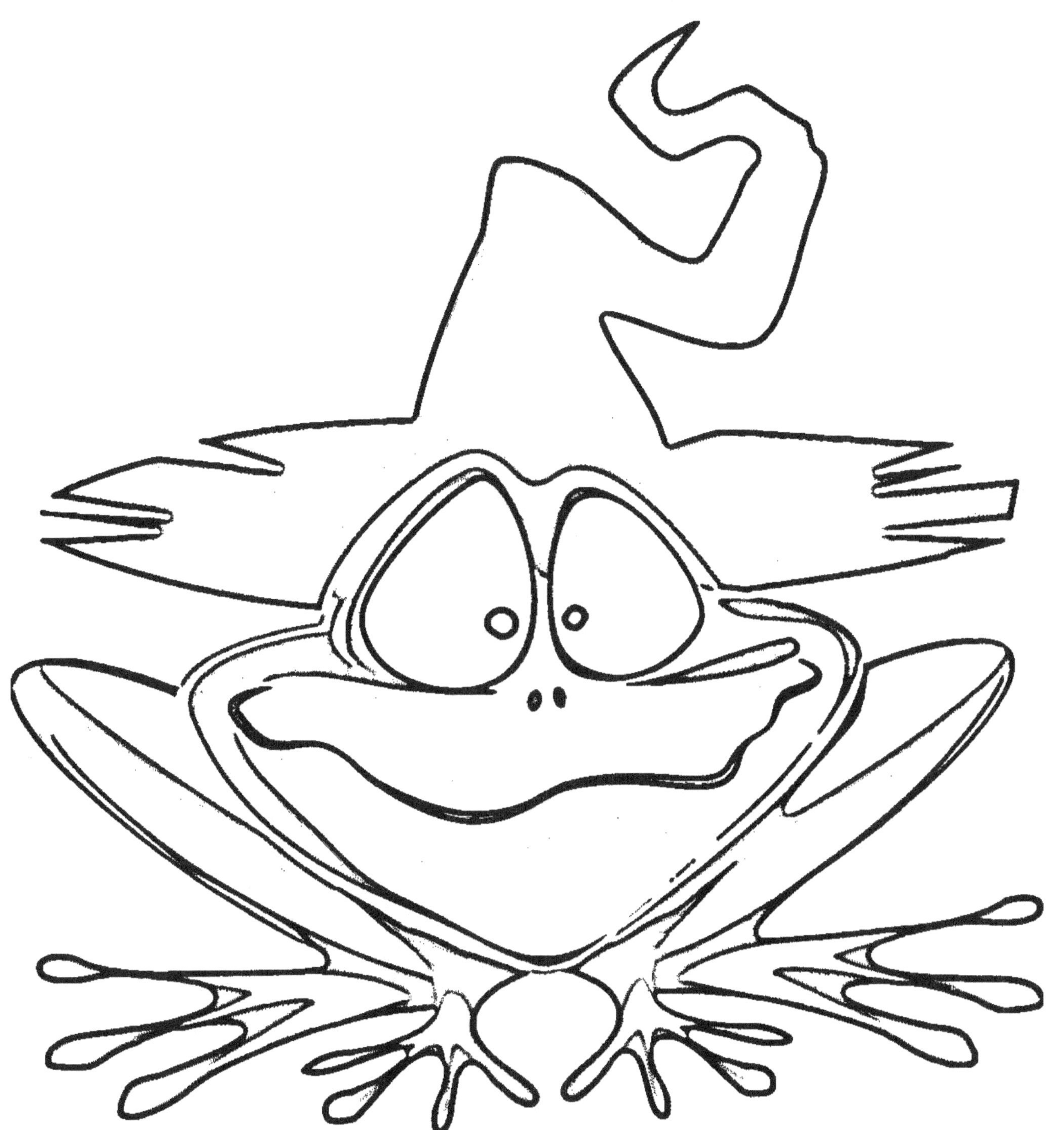

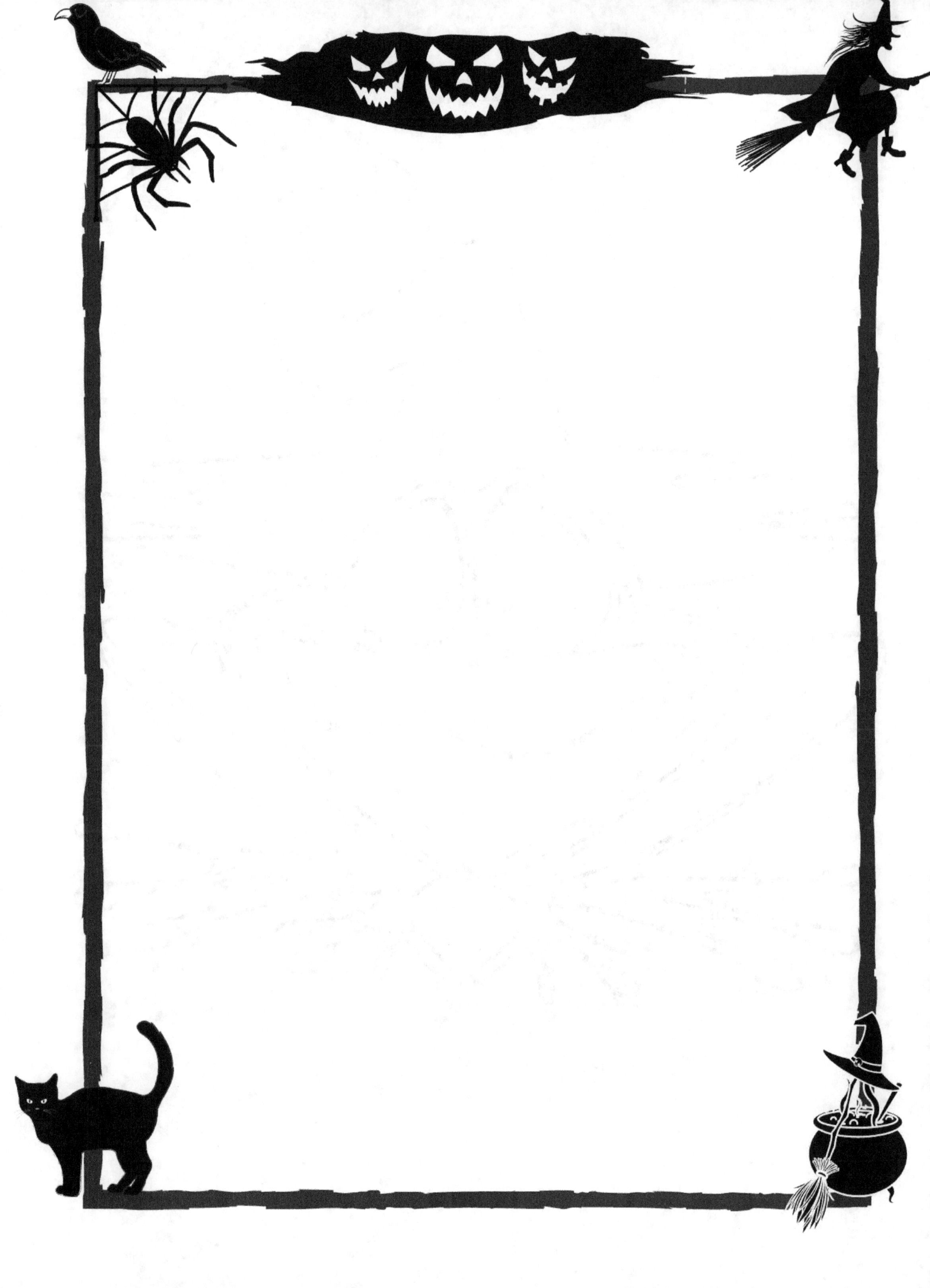

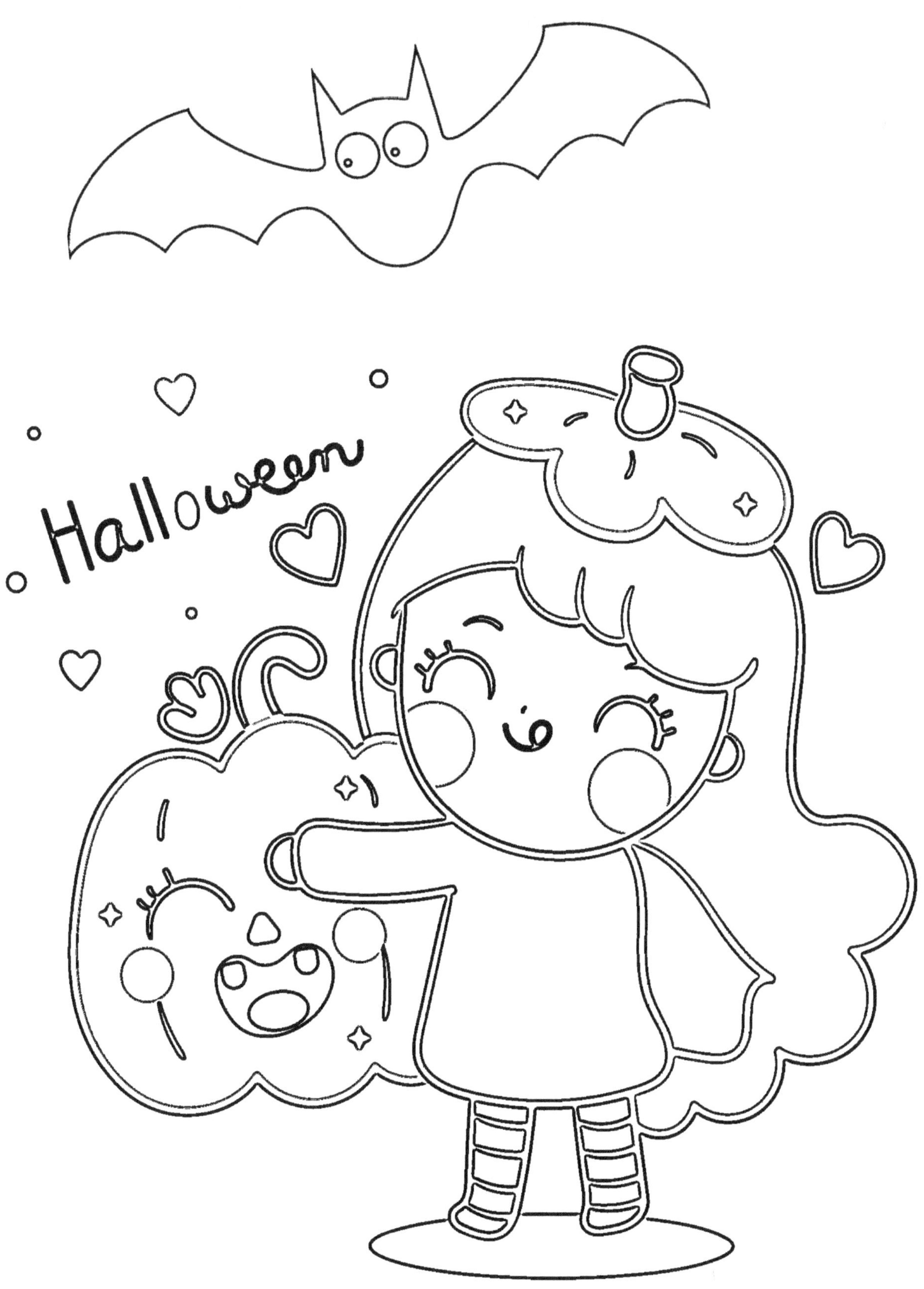
Halloween

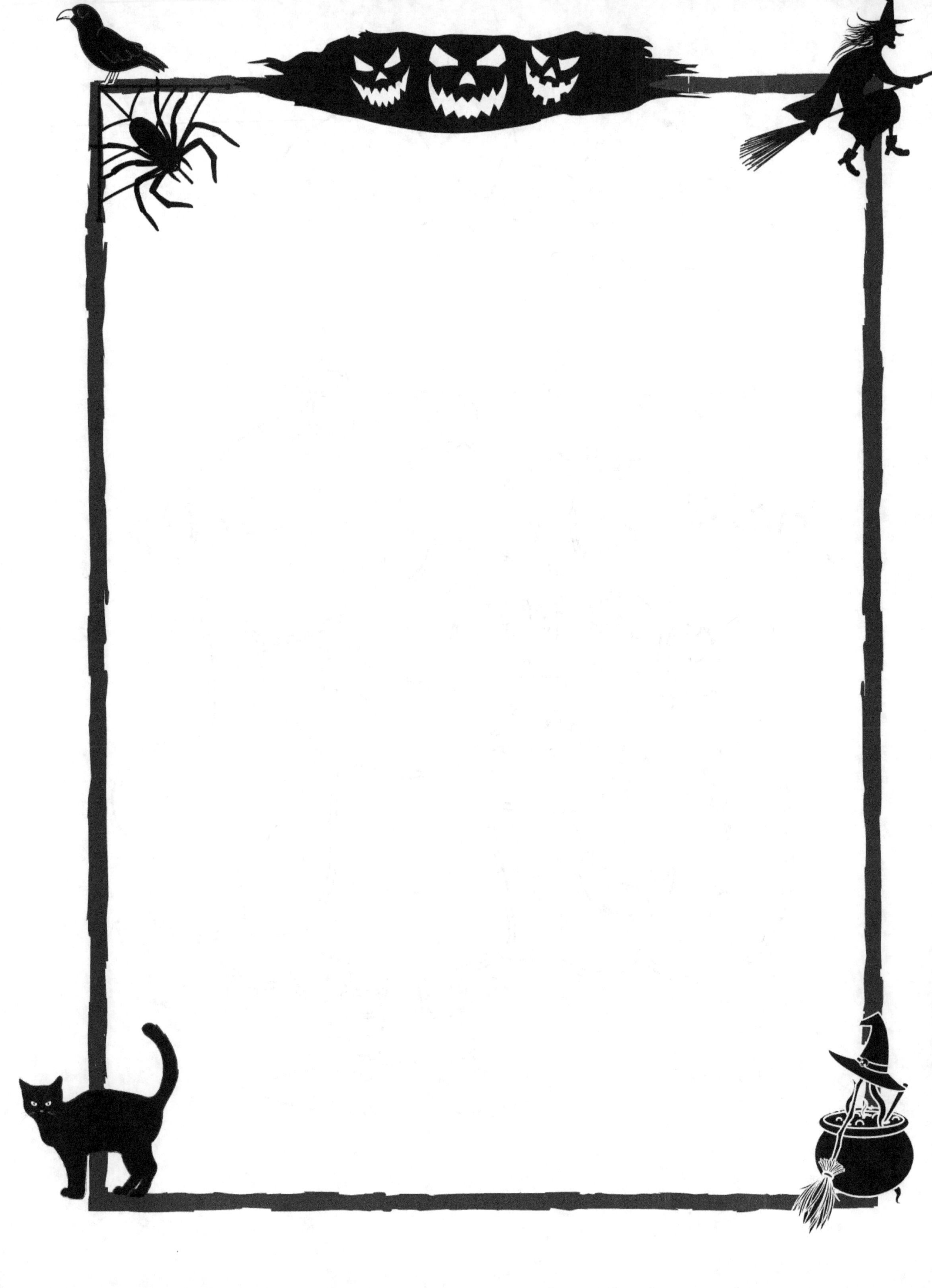

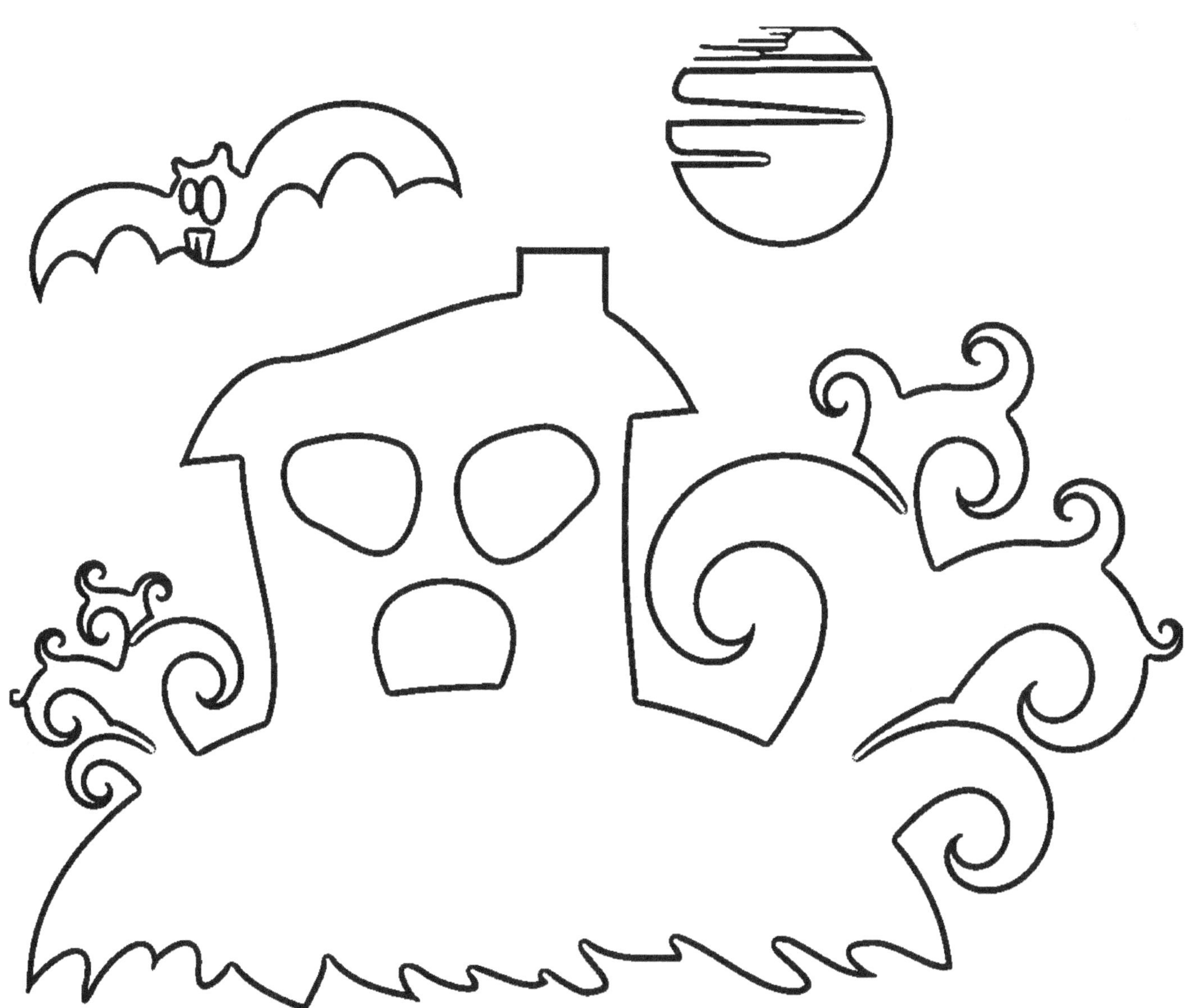

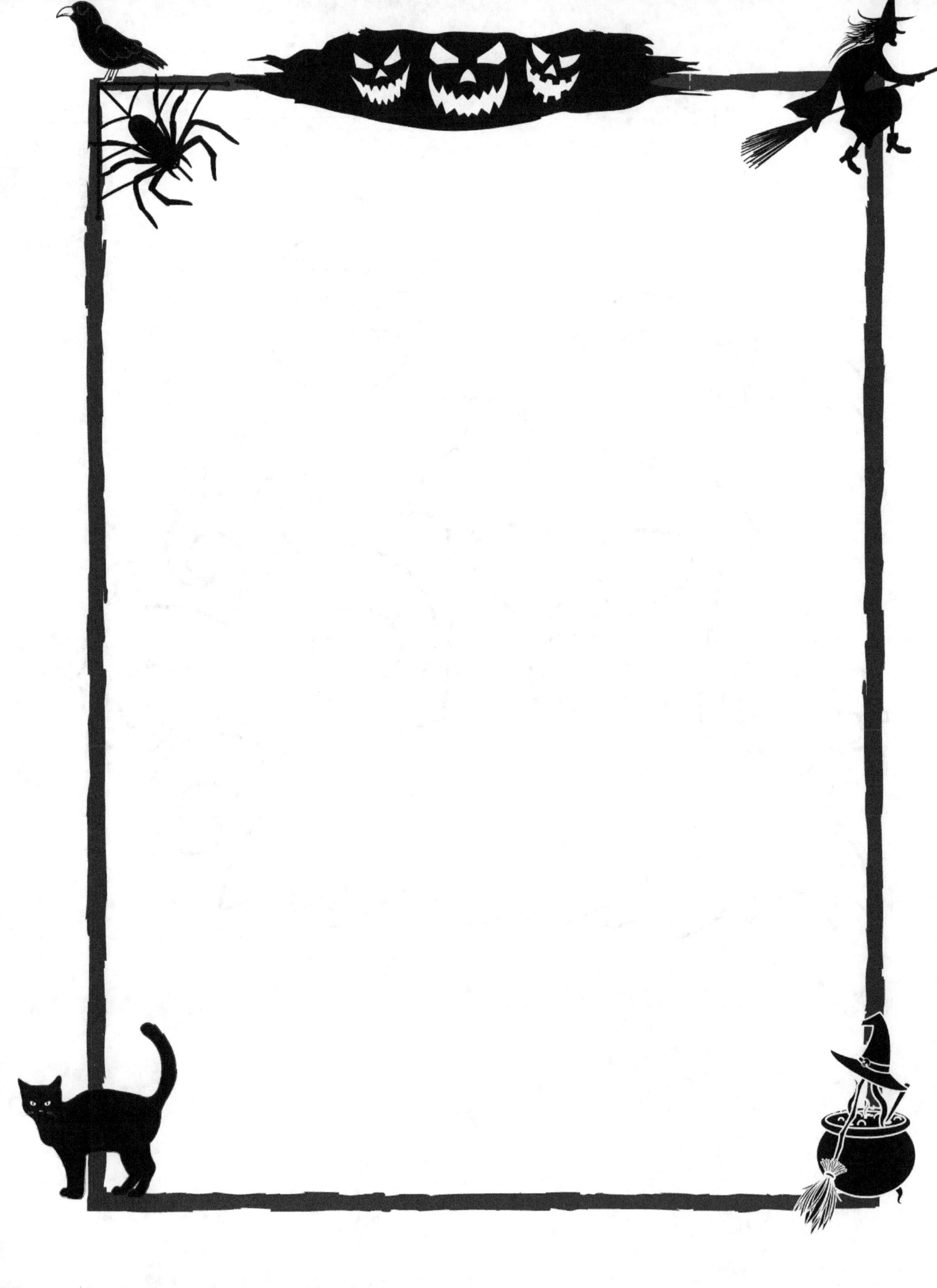

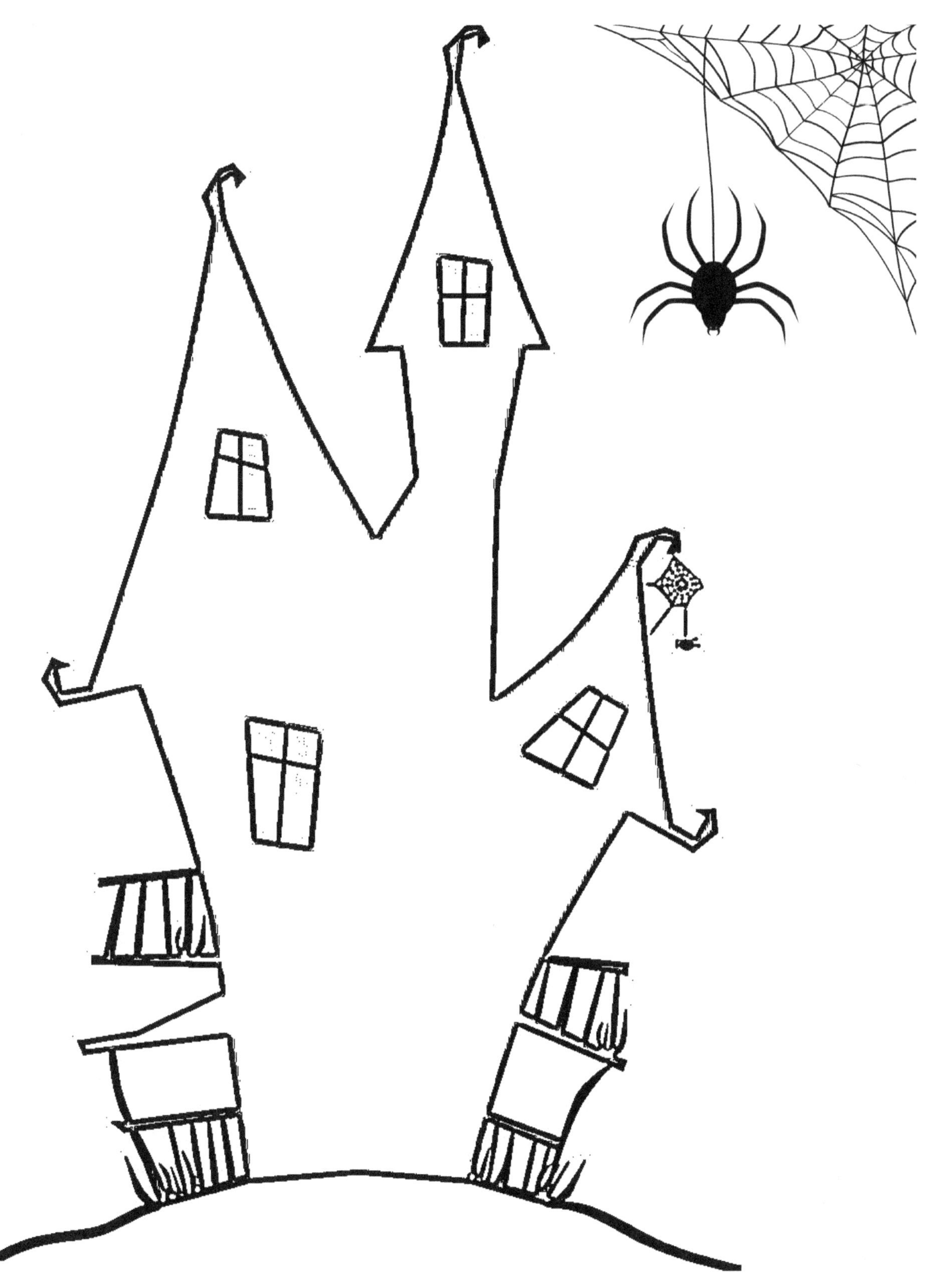

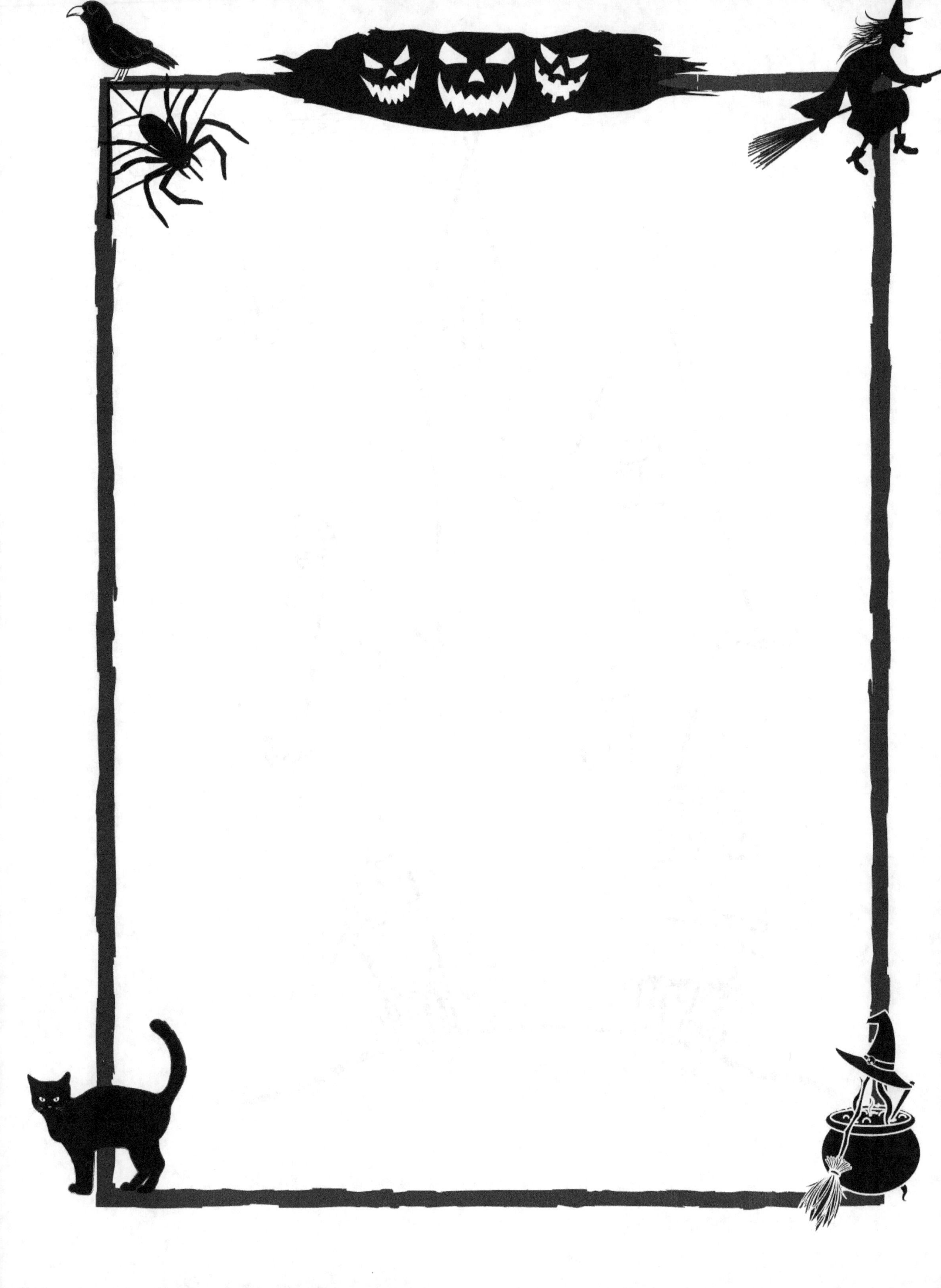

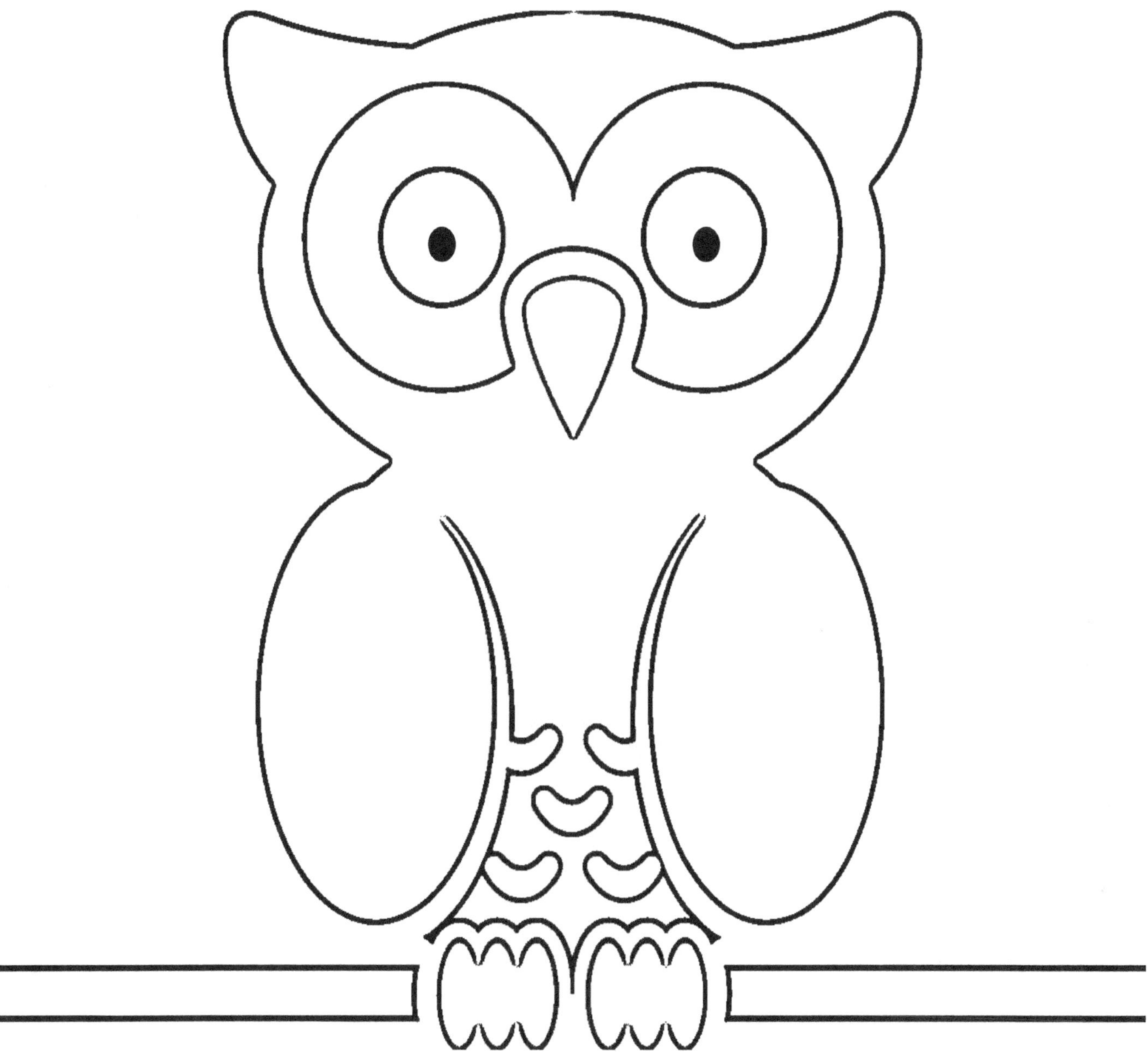

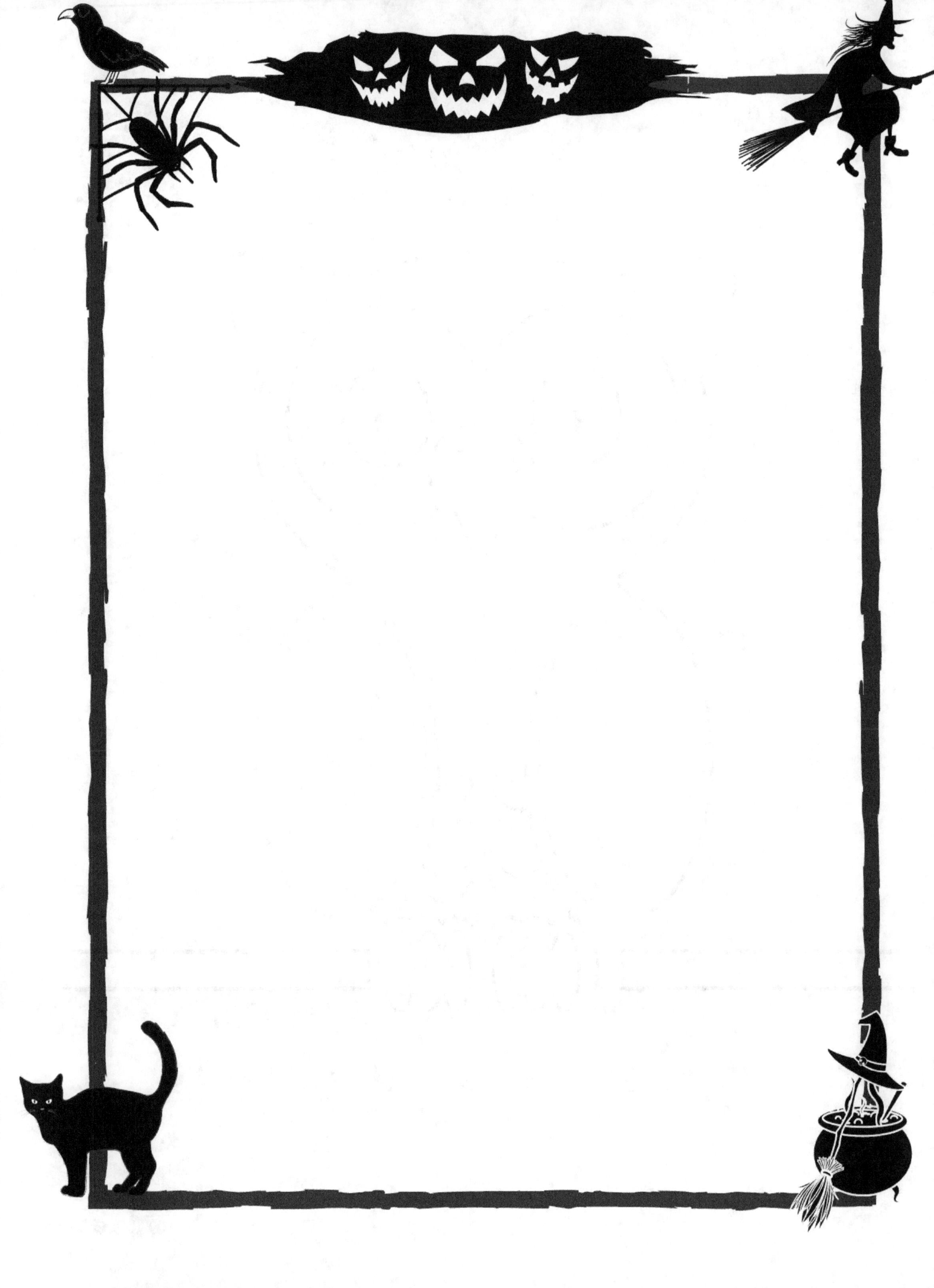

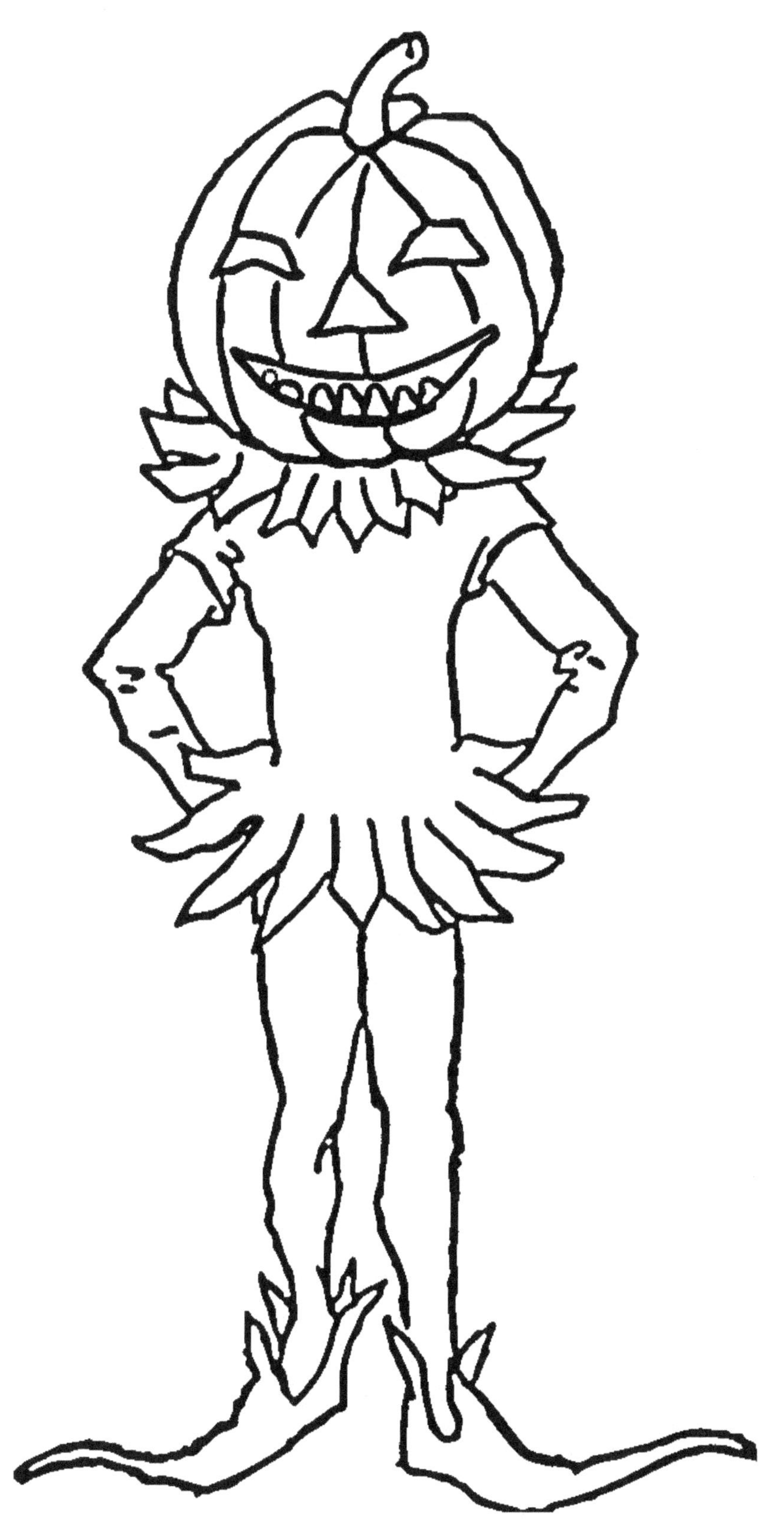

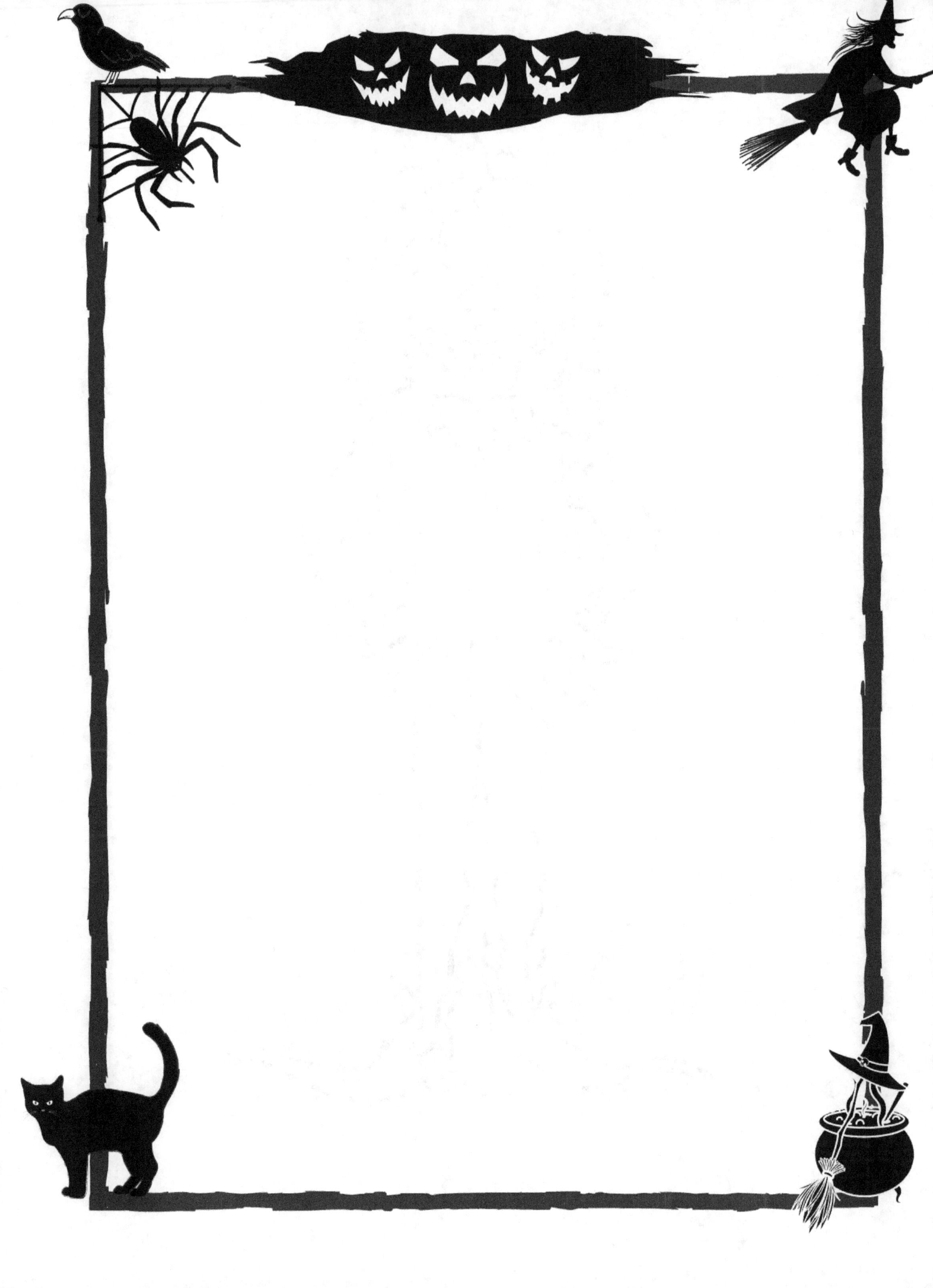

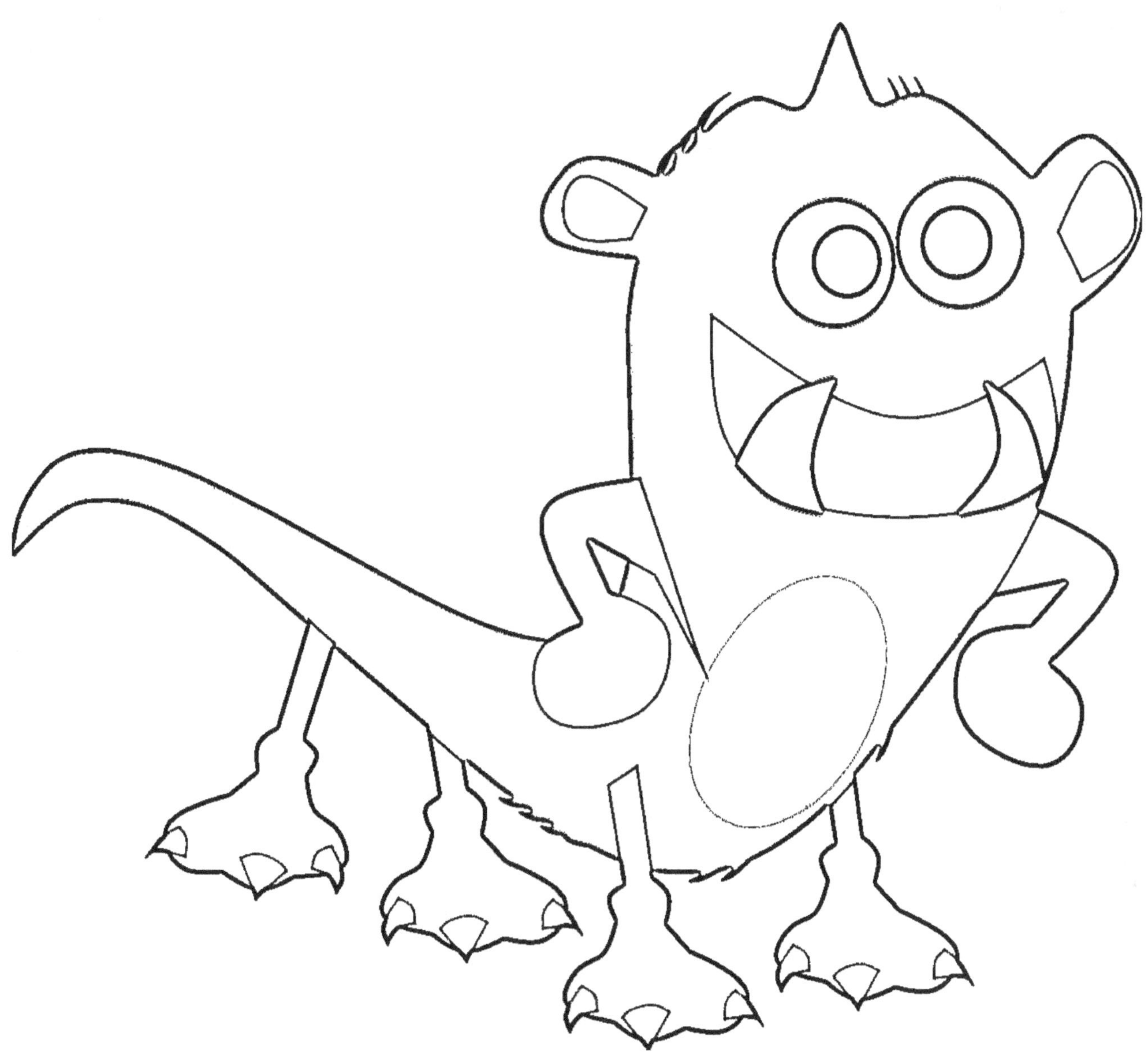

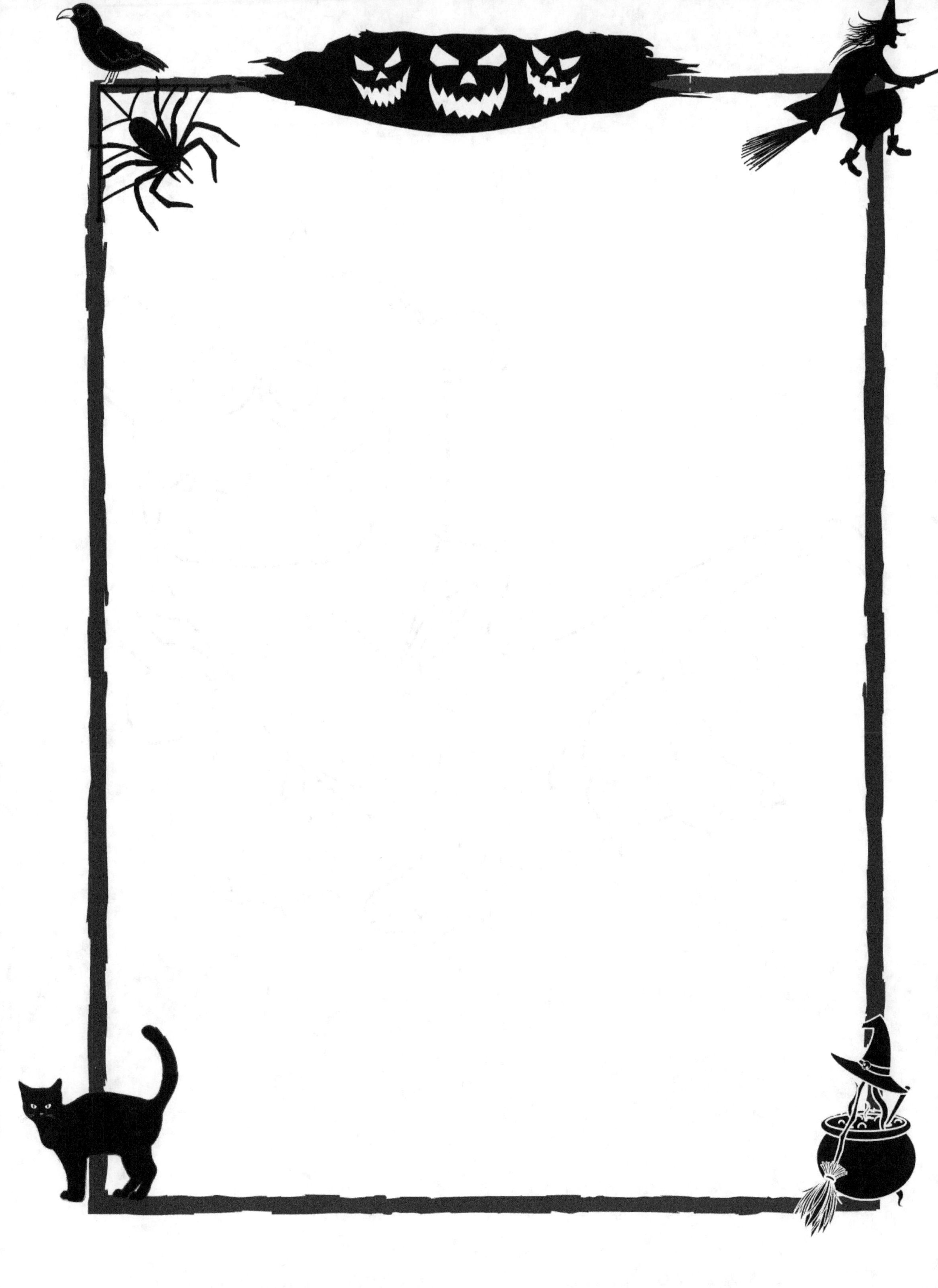

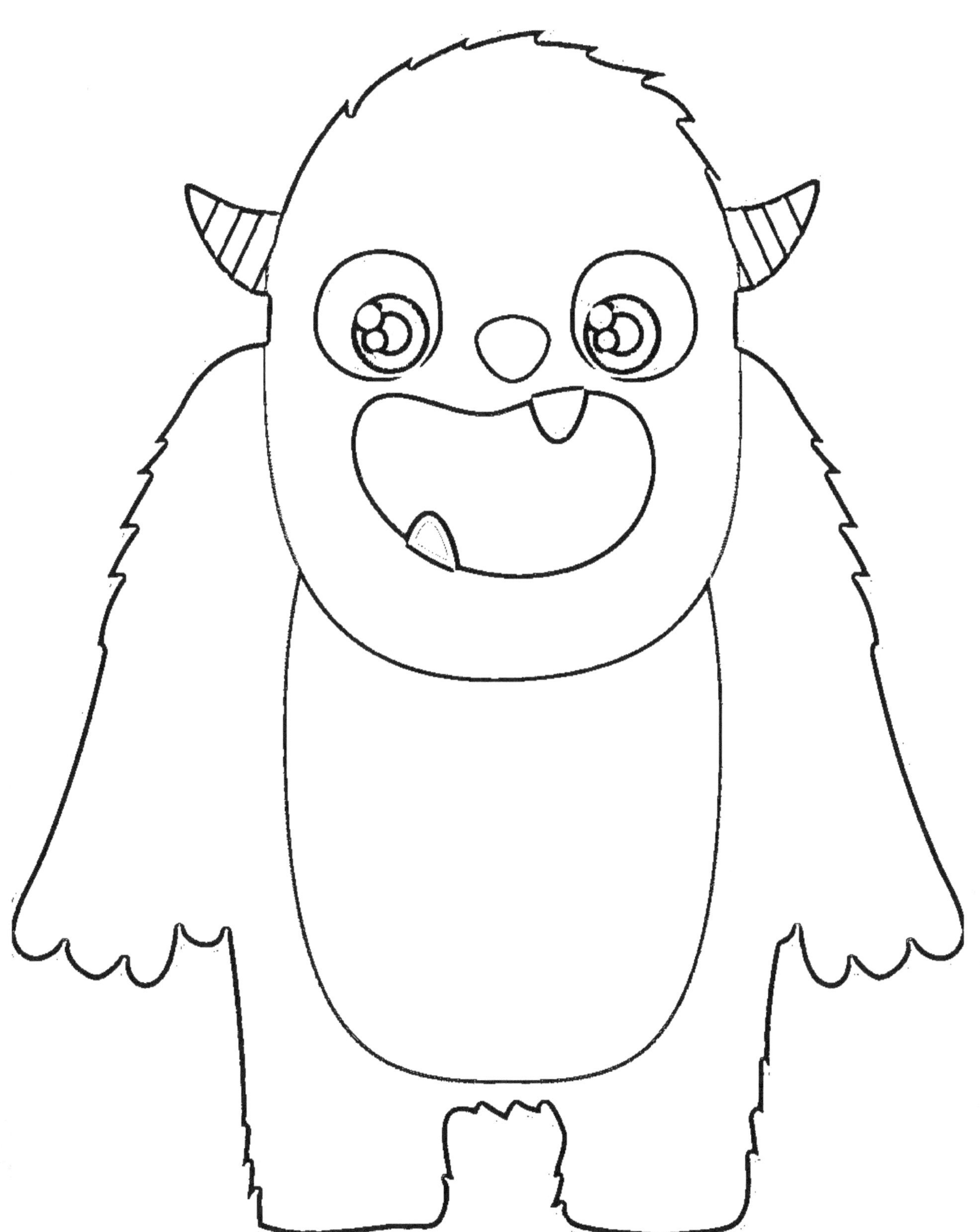

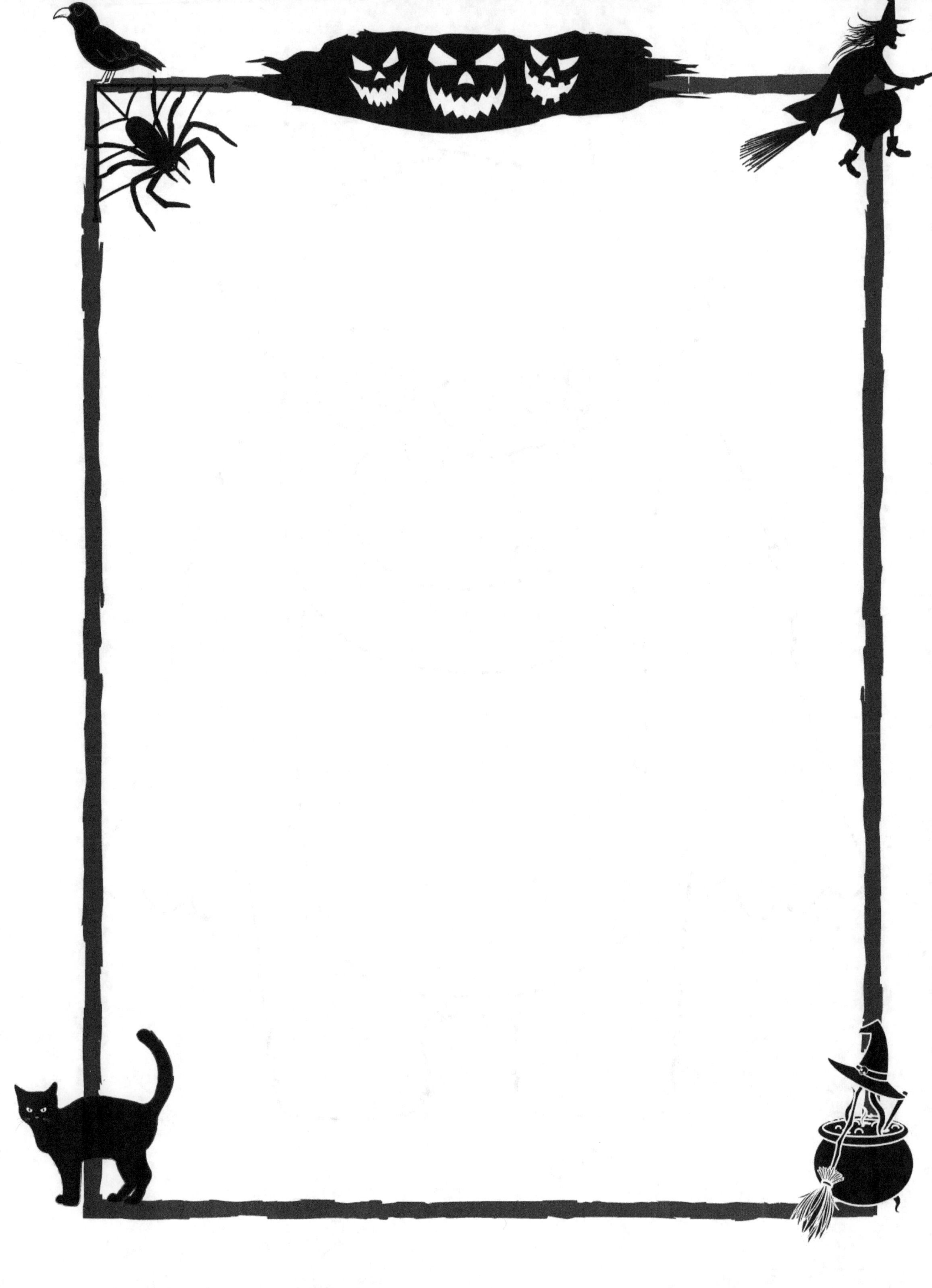

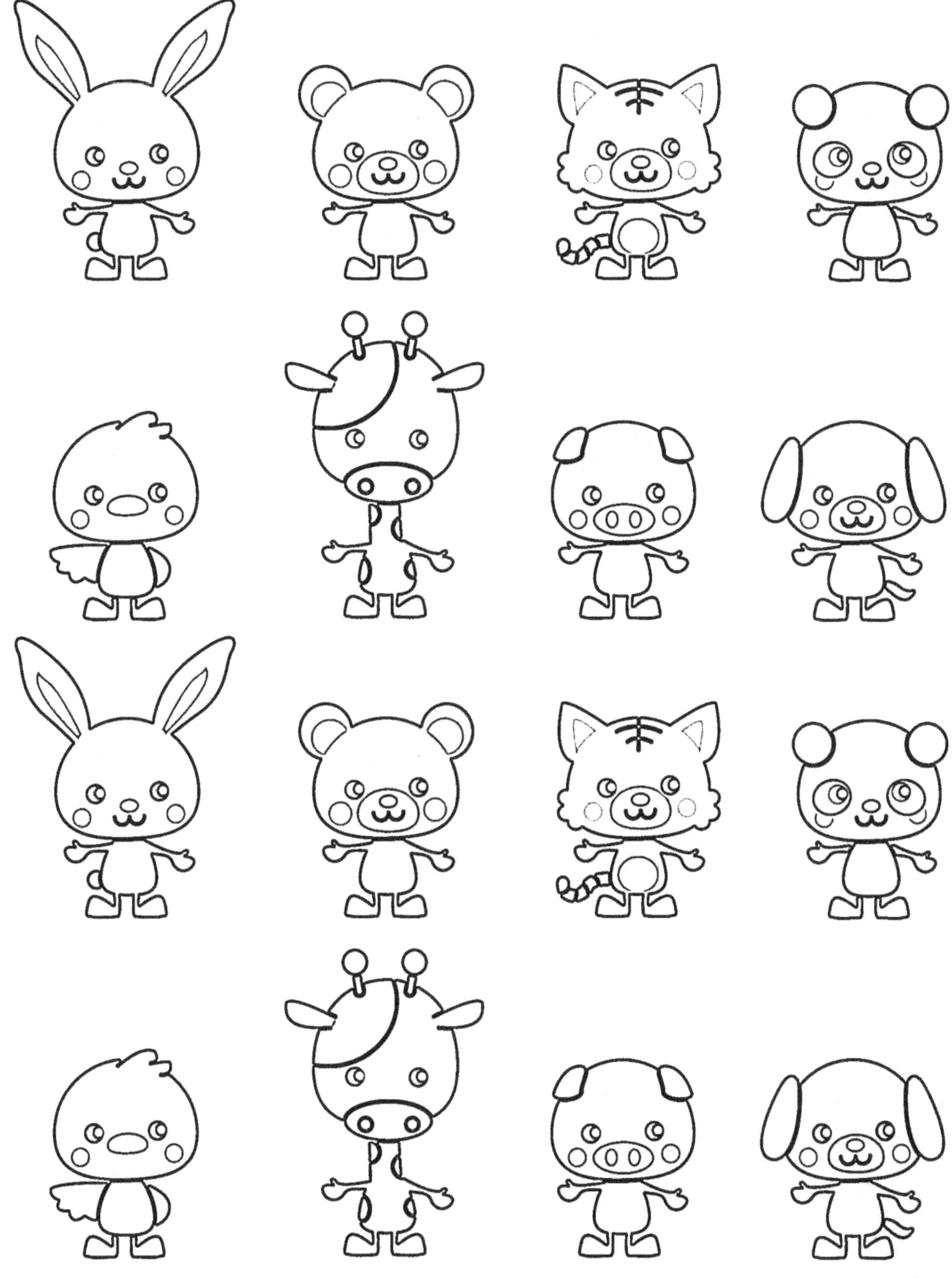

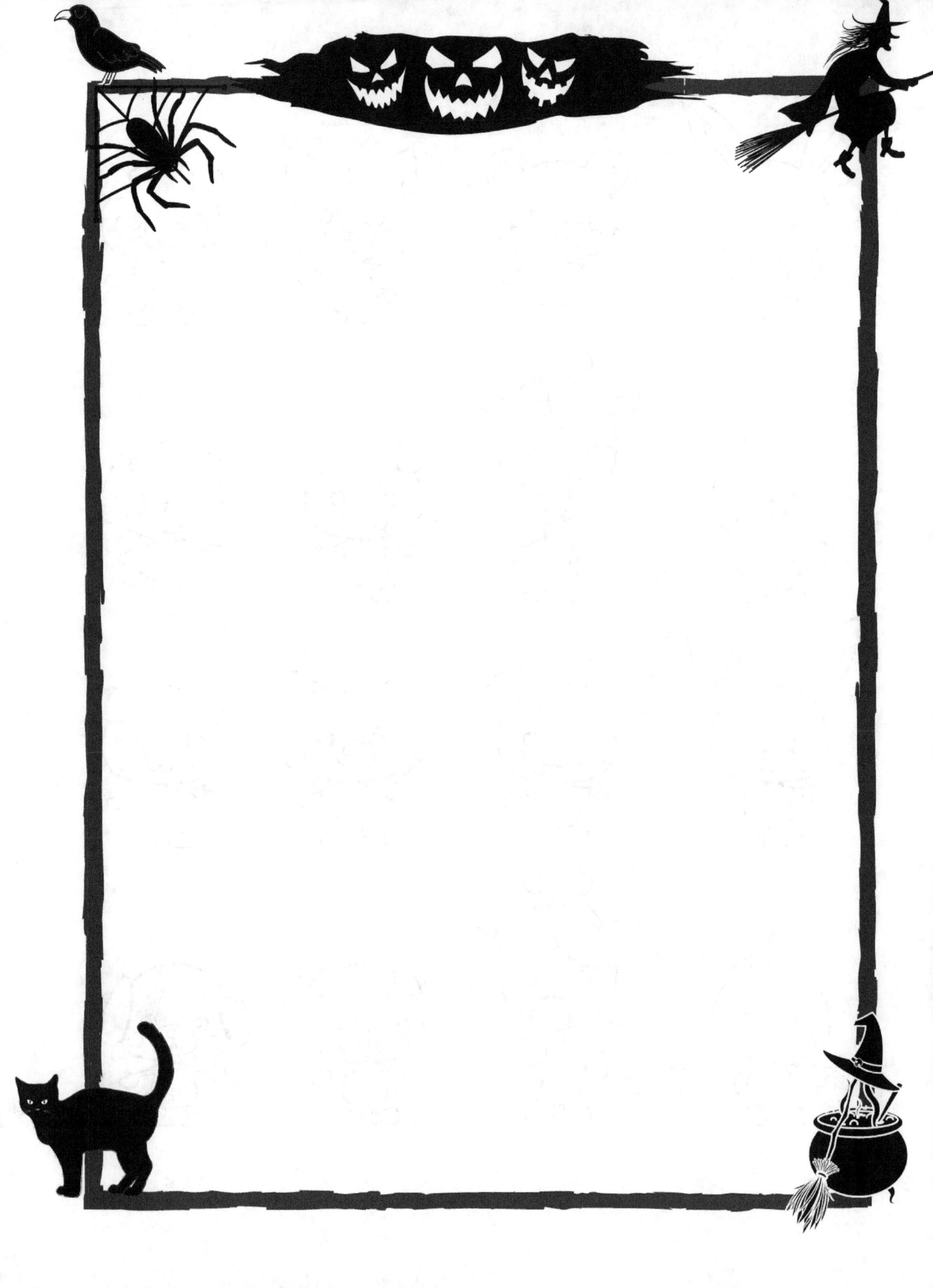

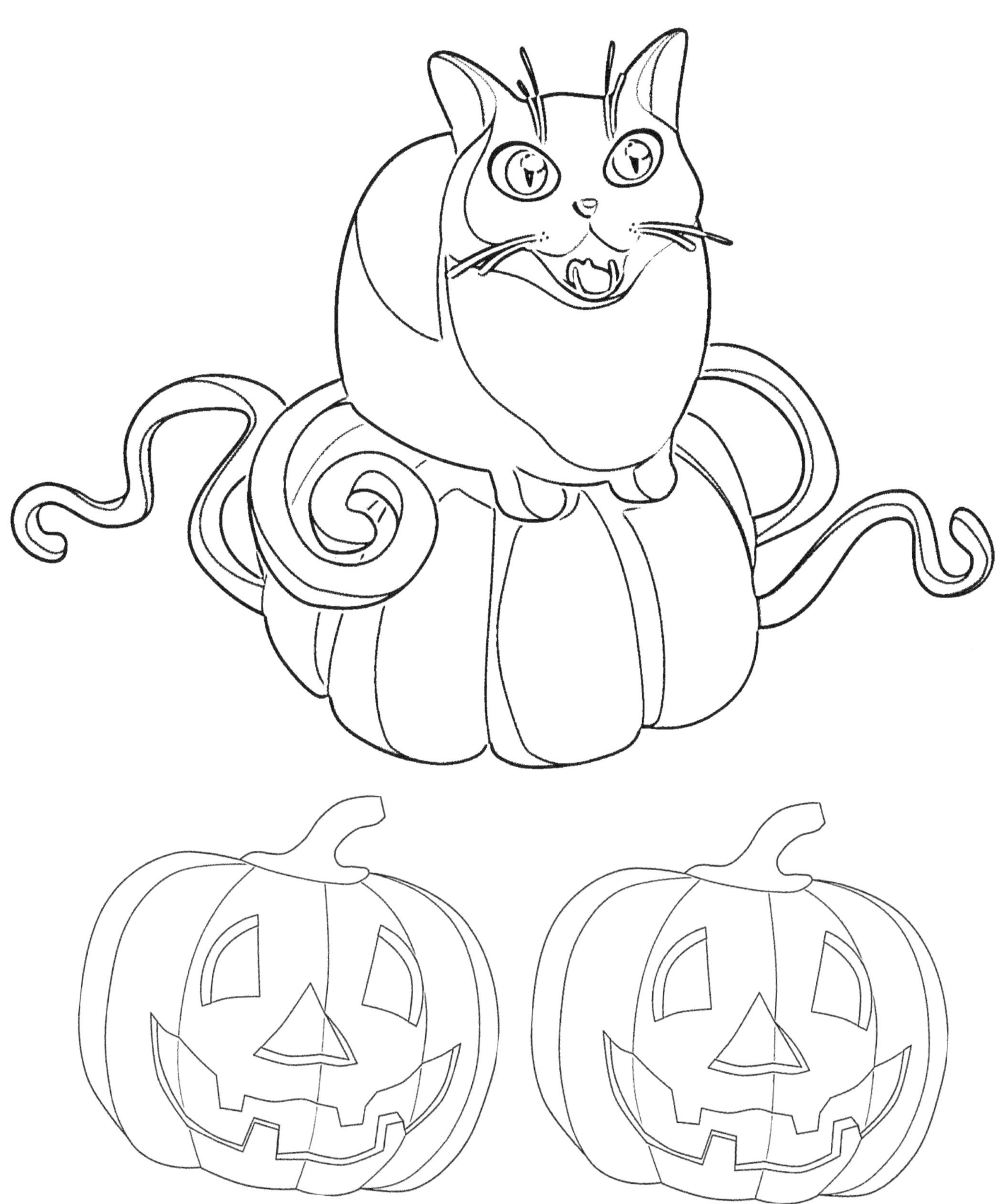

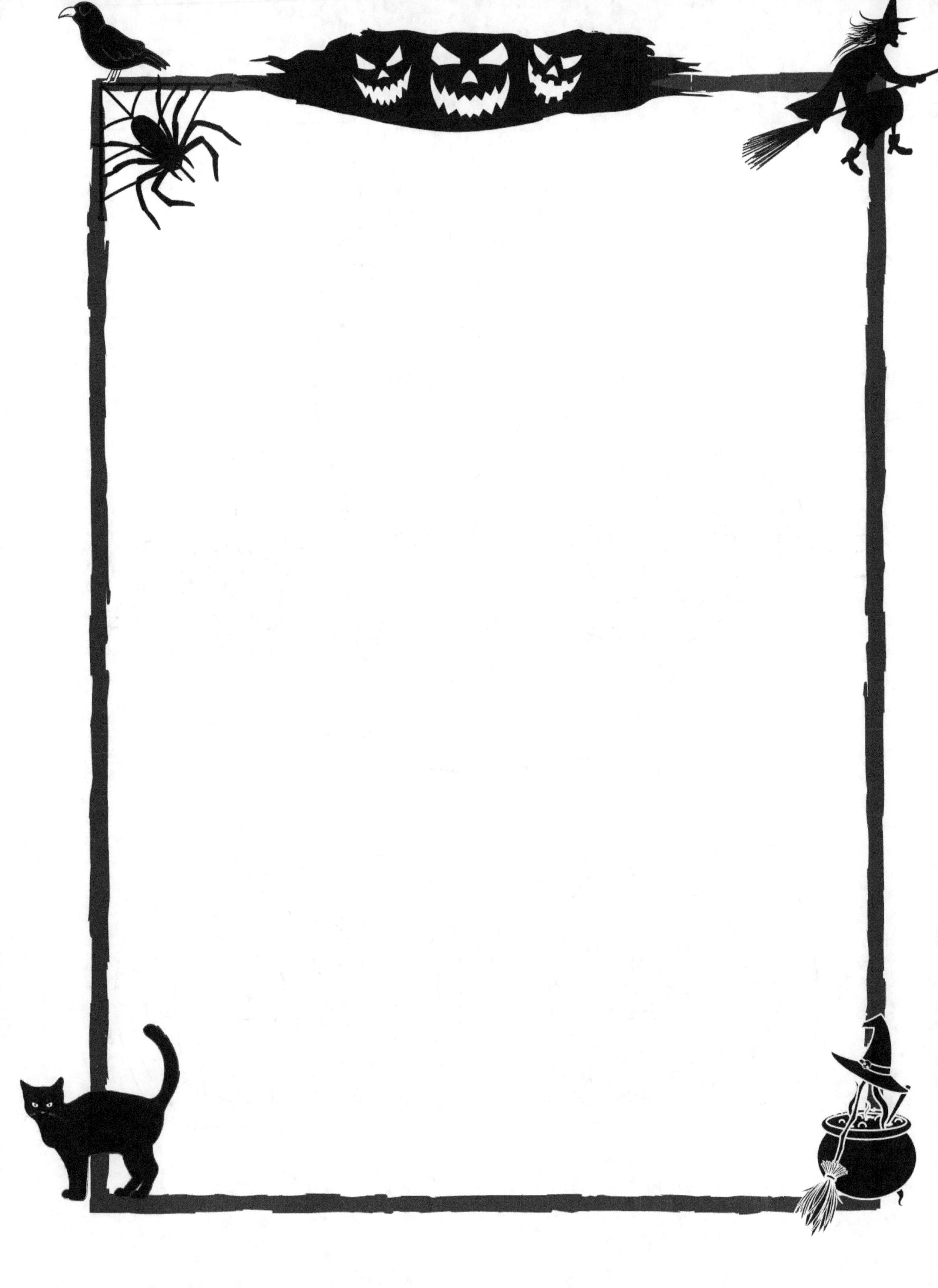

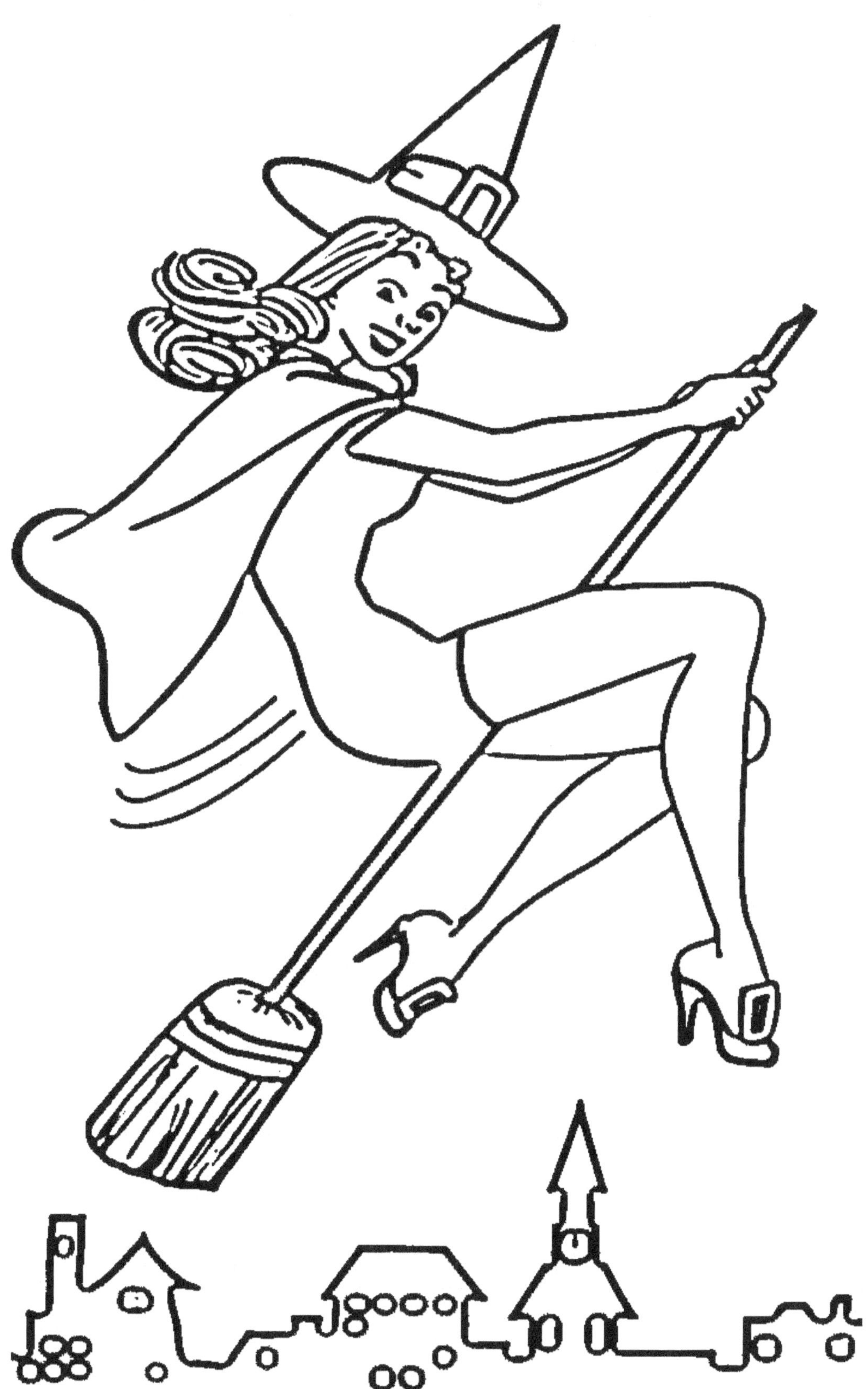

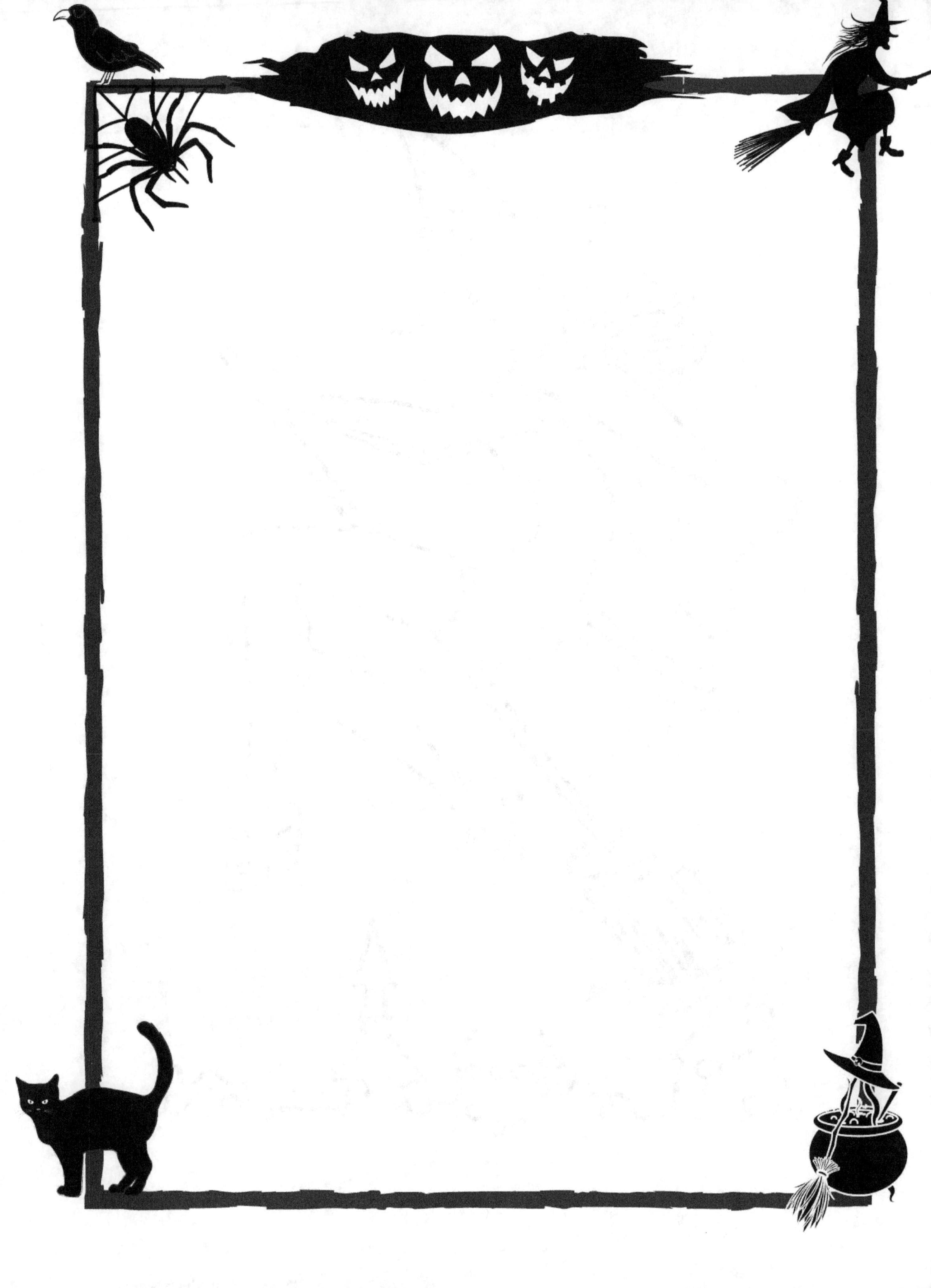

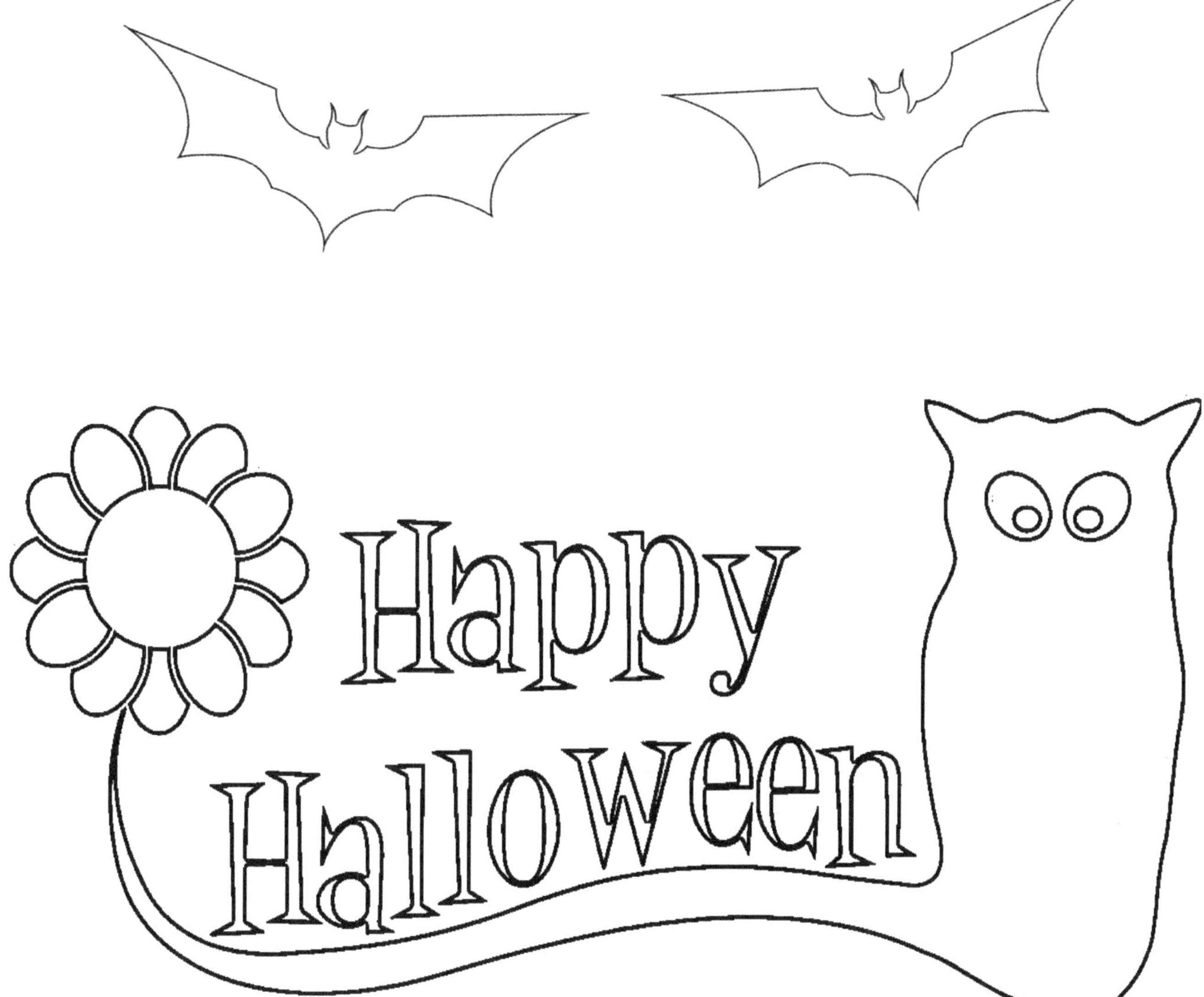

Happy
Halloween

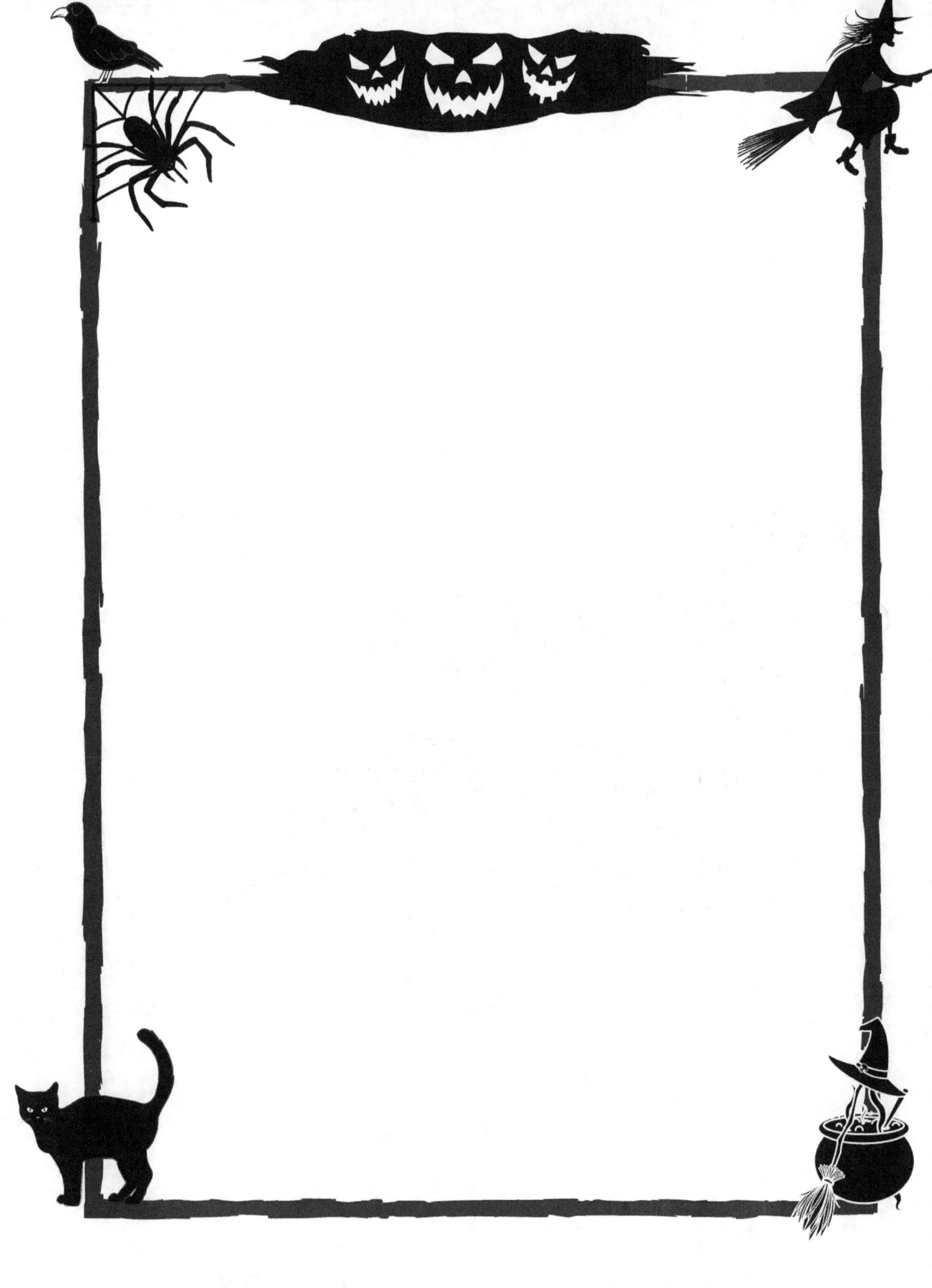

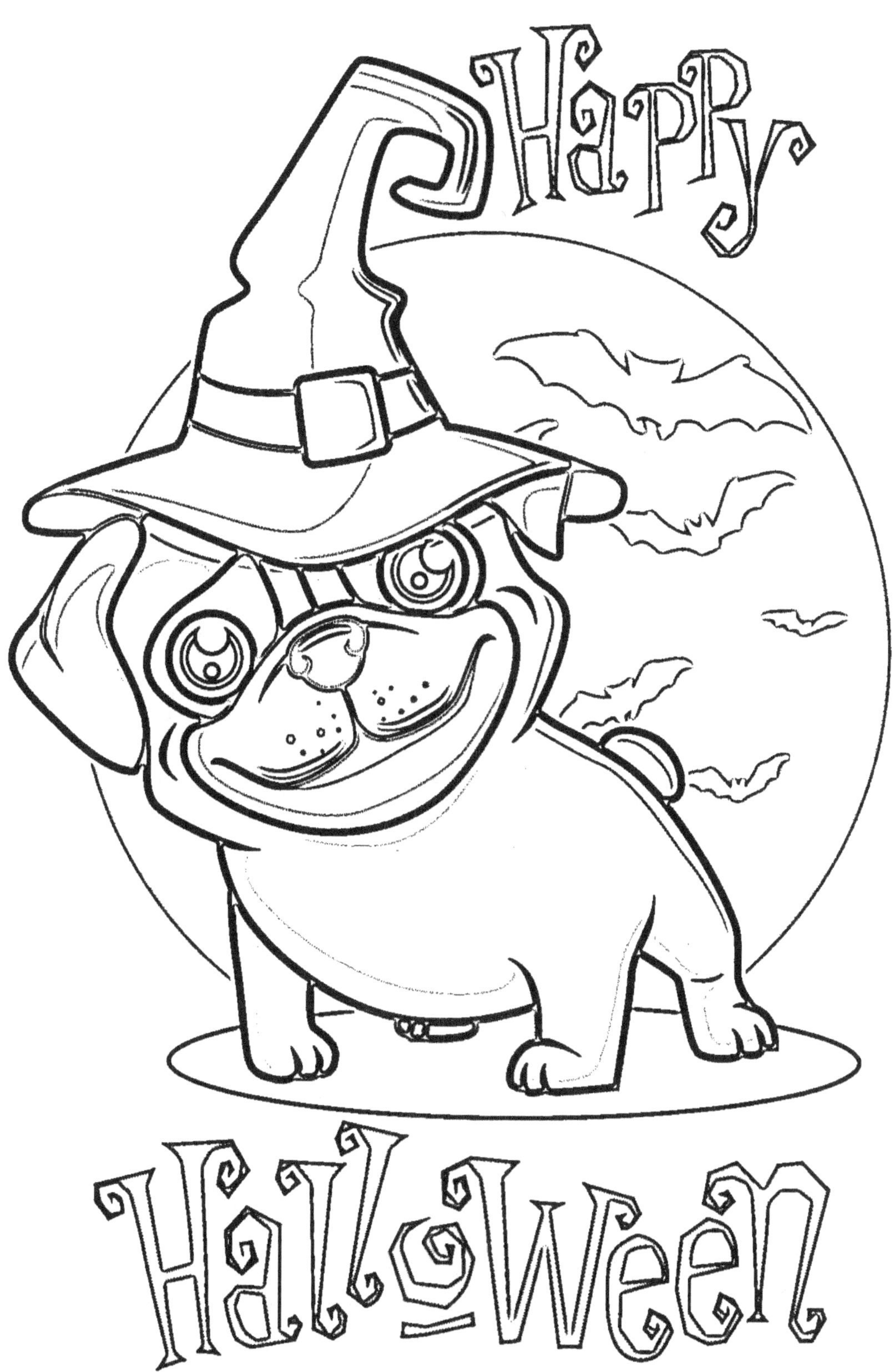

Happy
Halloween

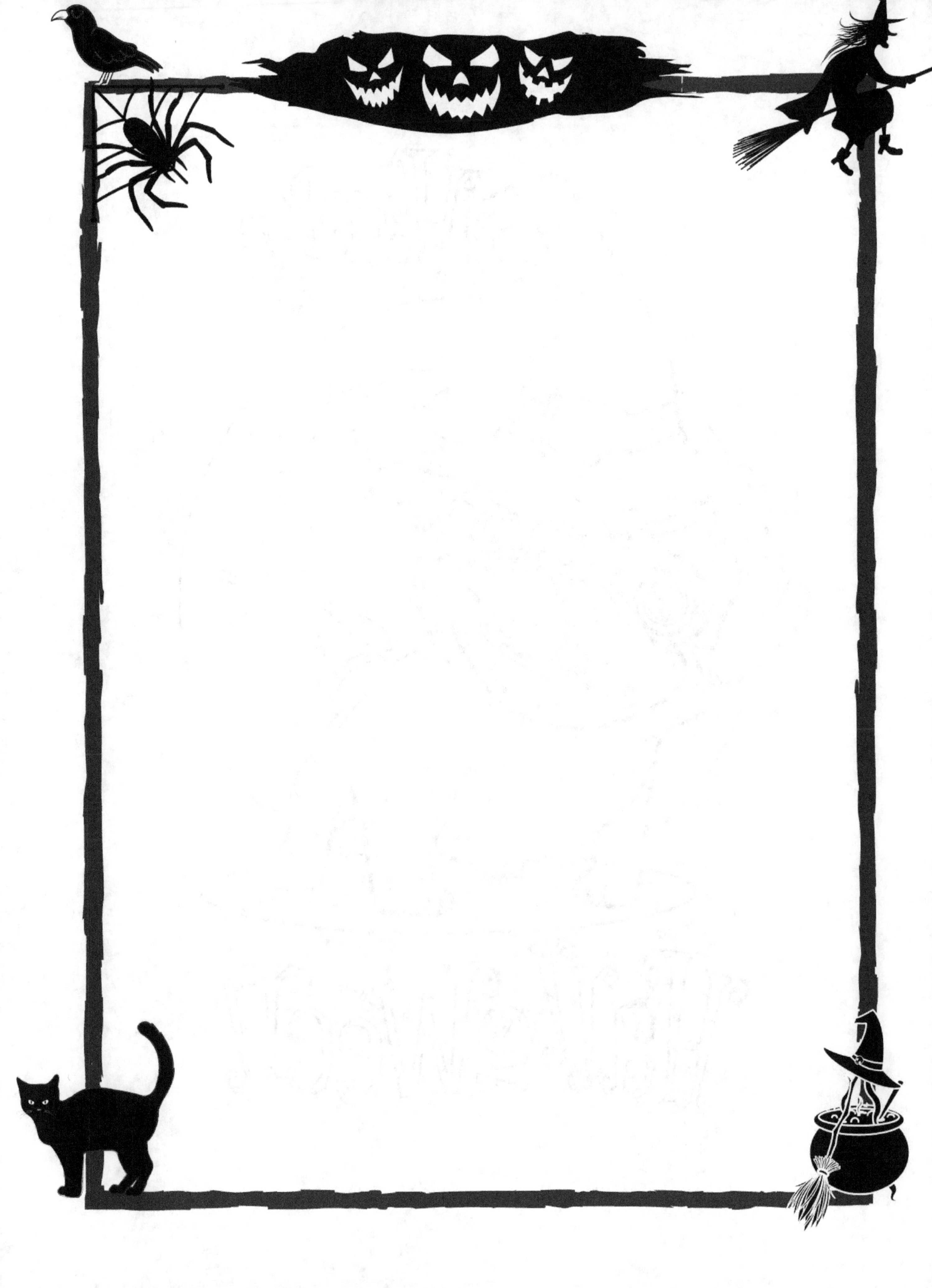

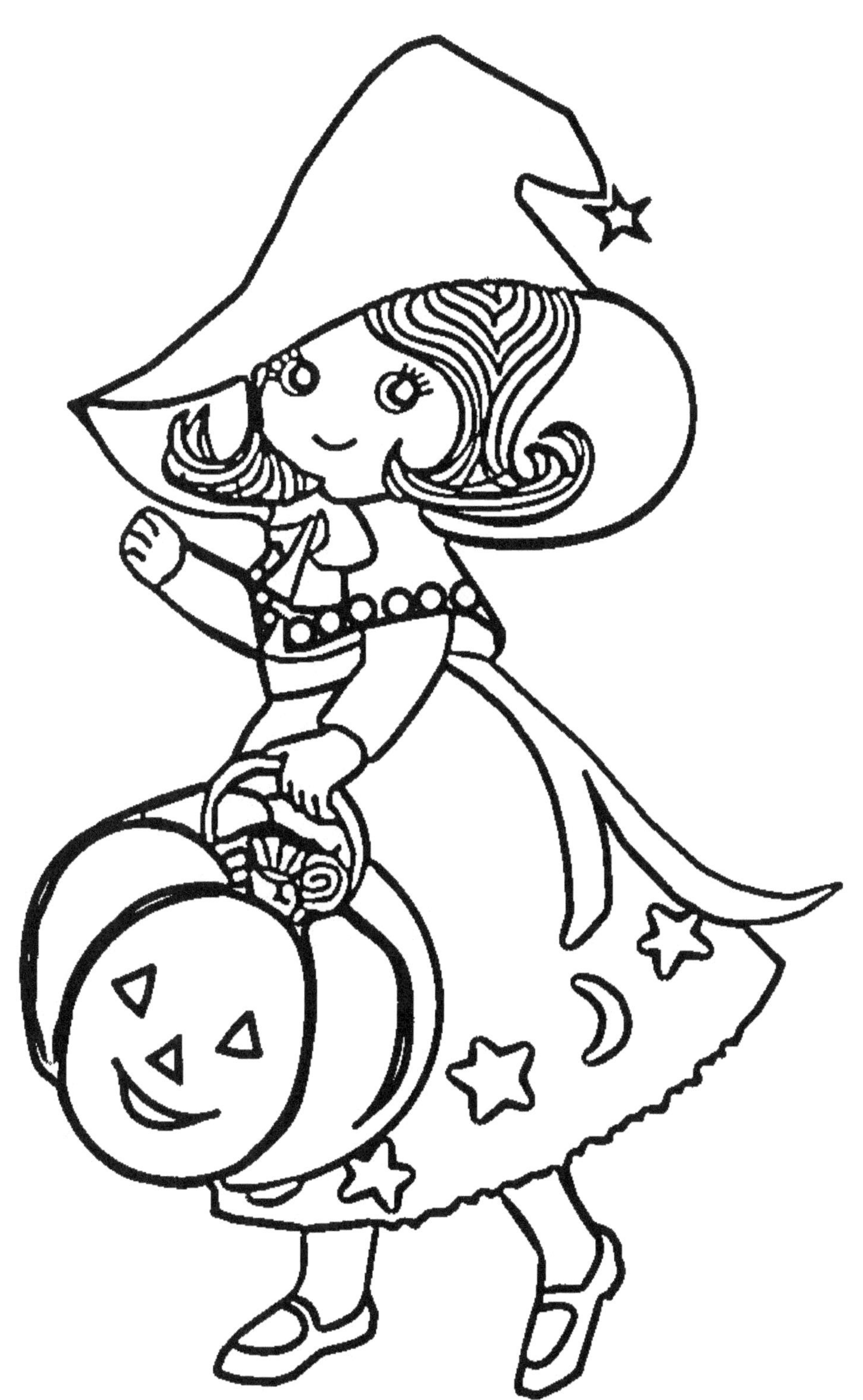

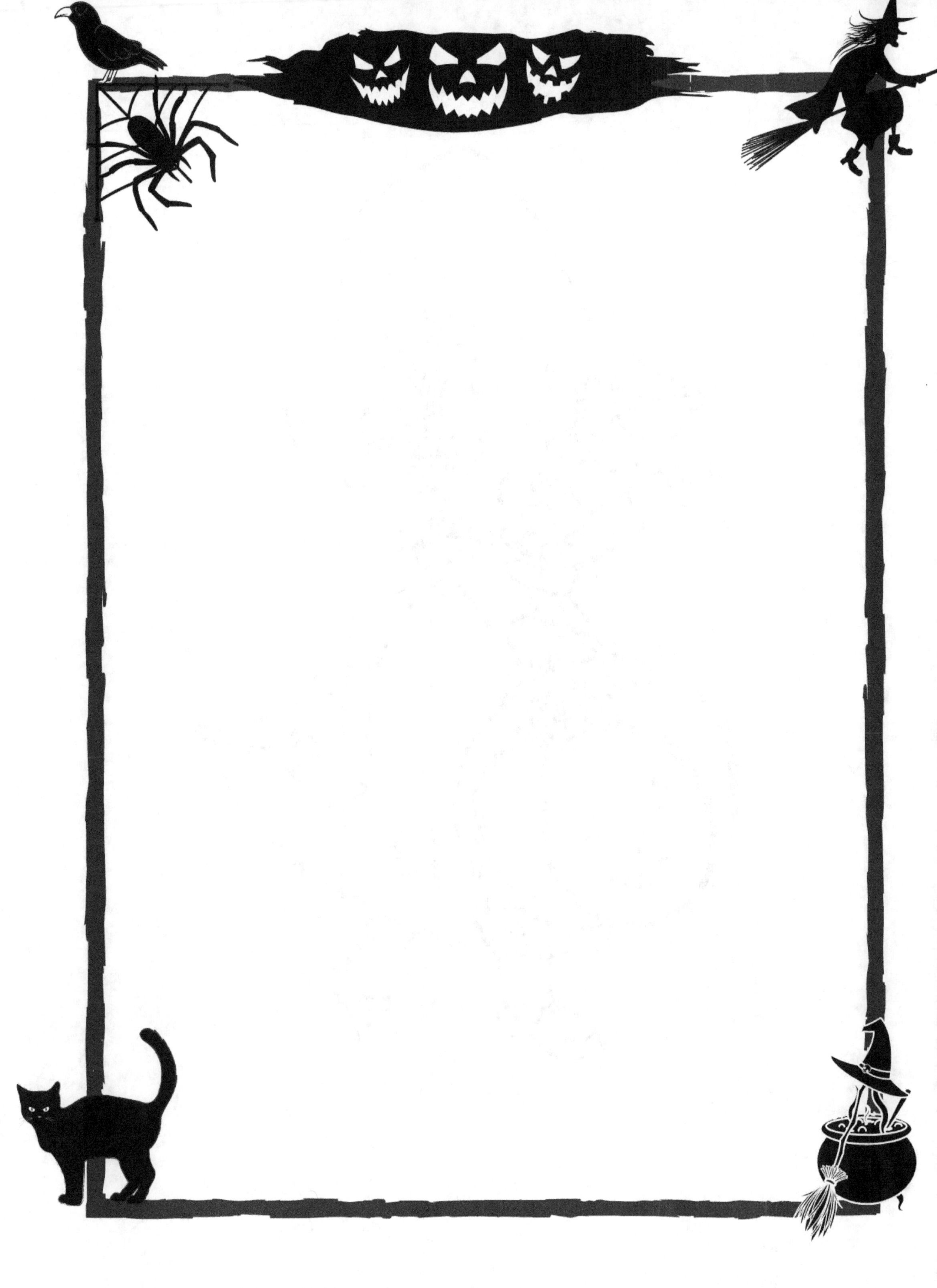

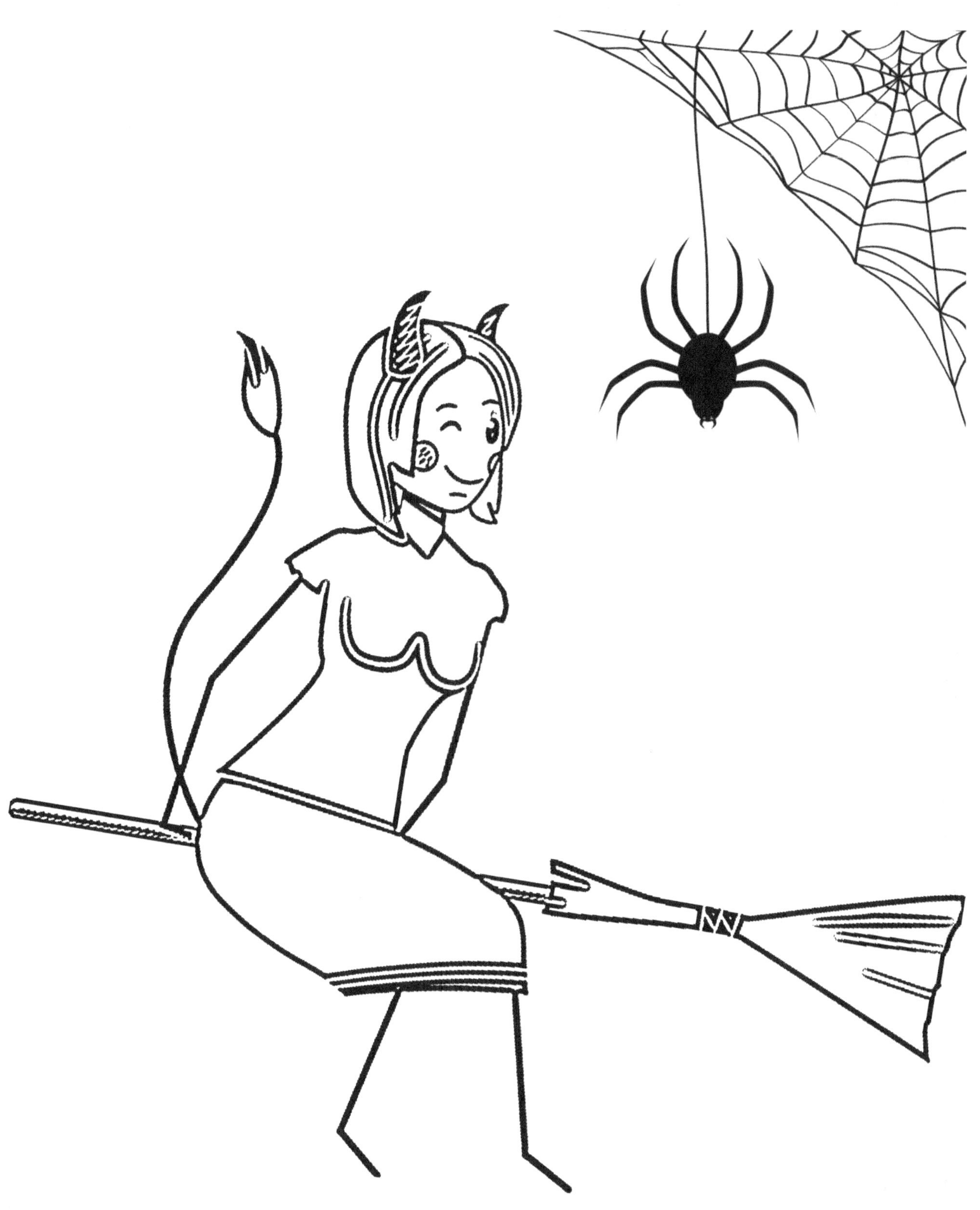

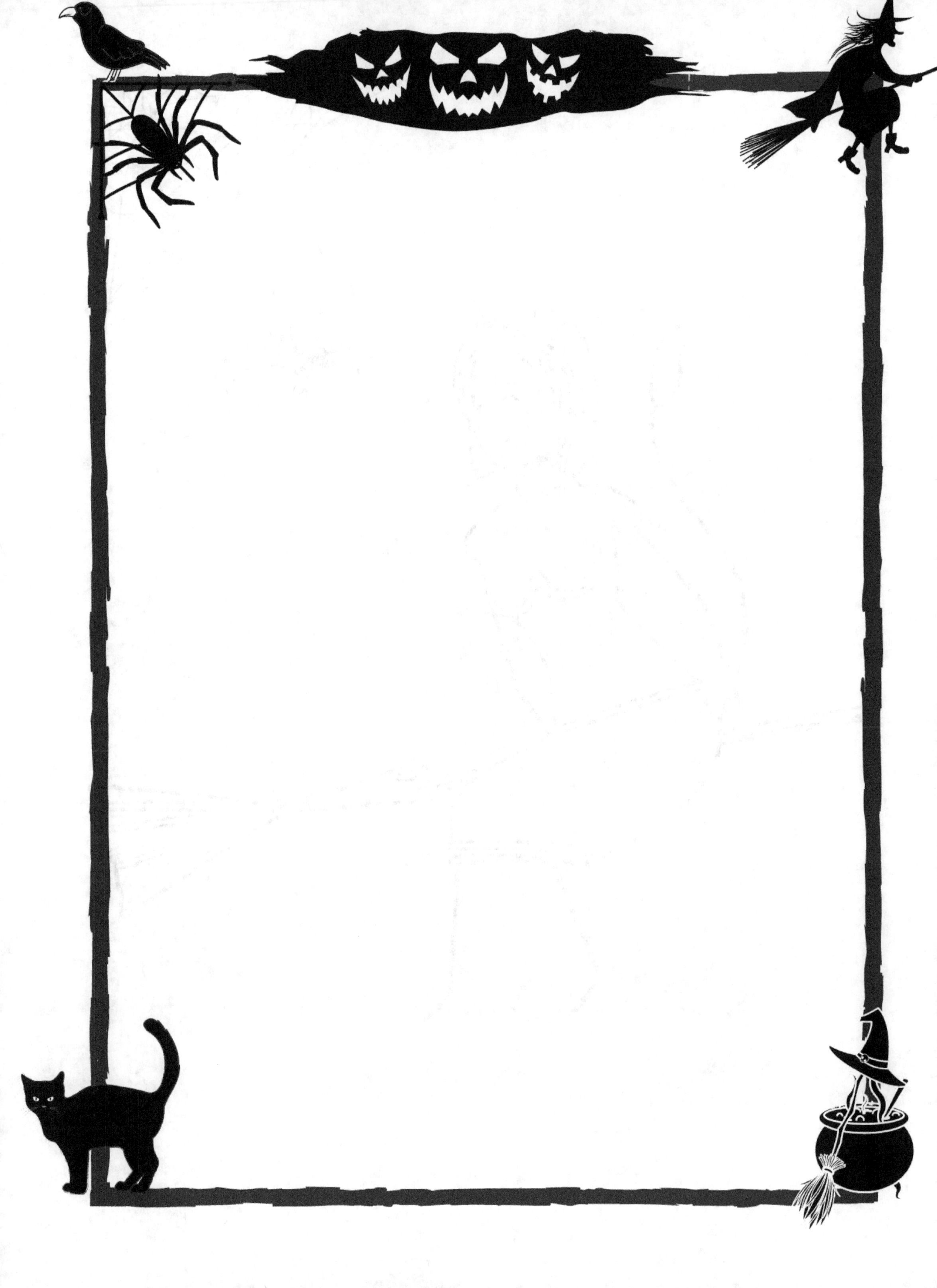

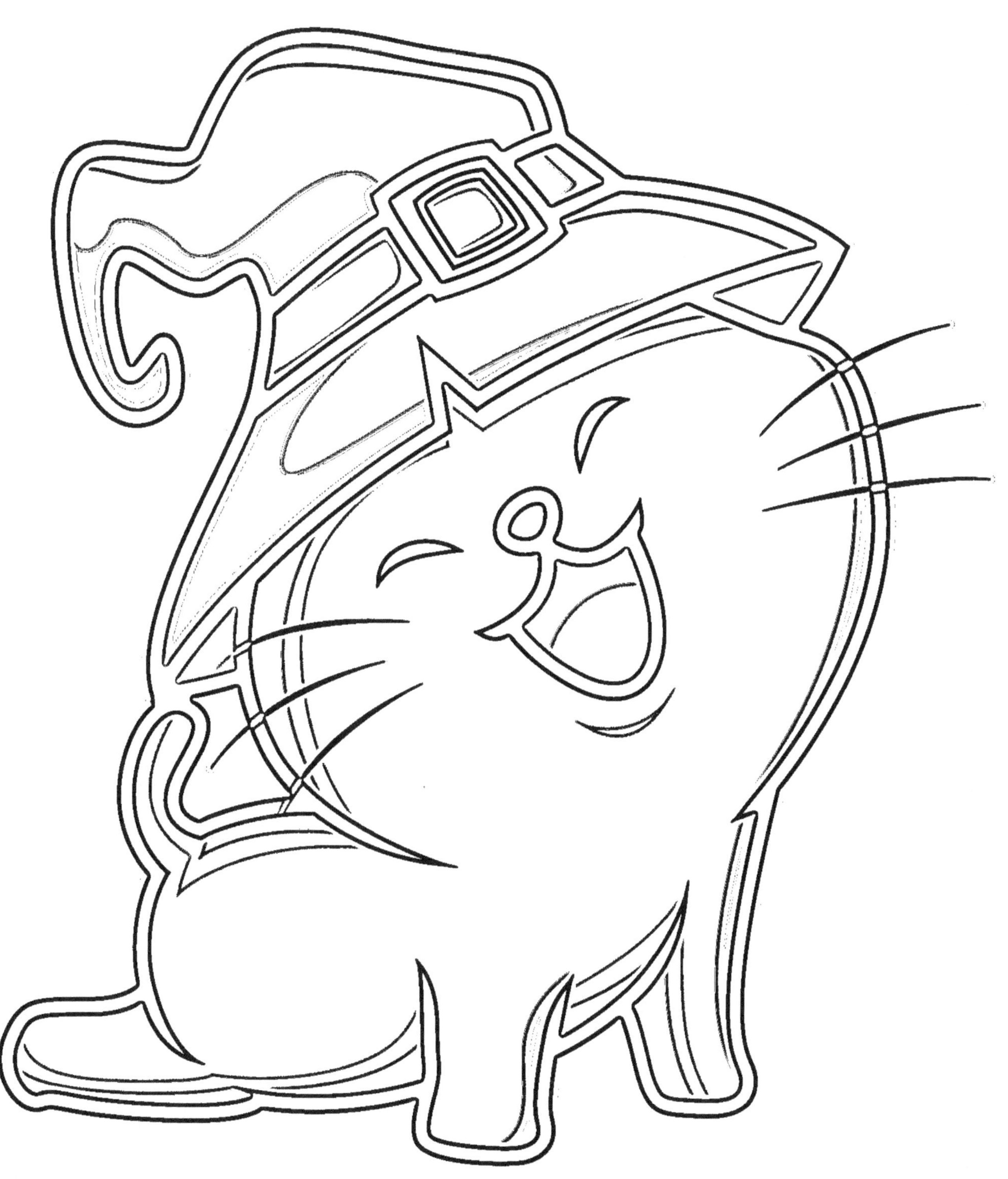

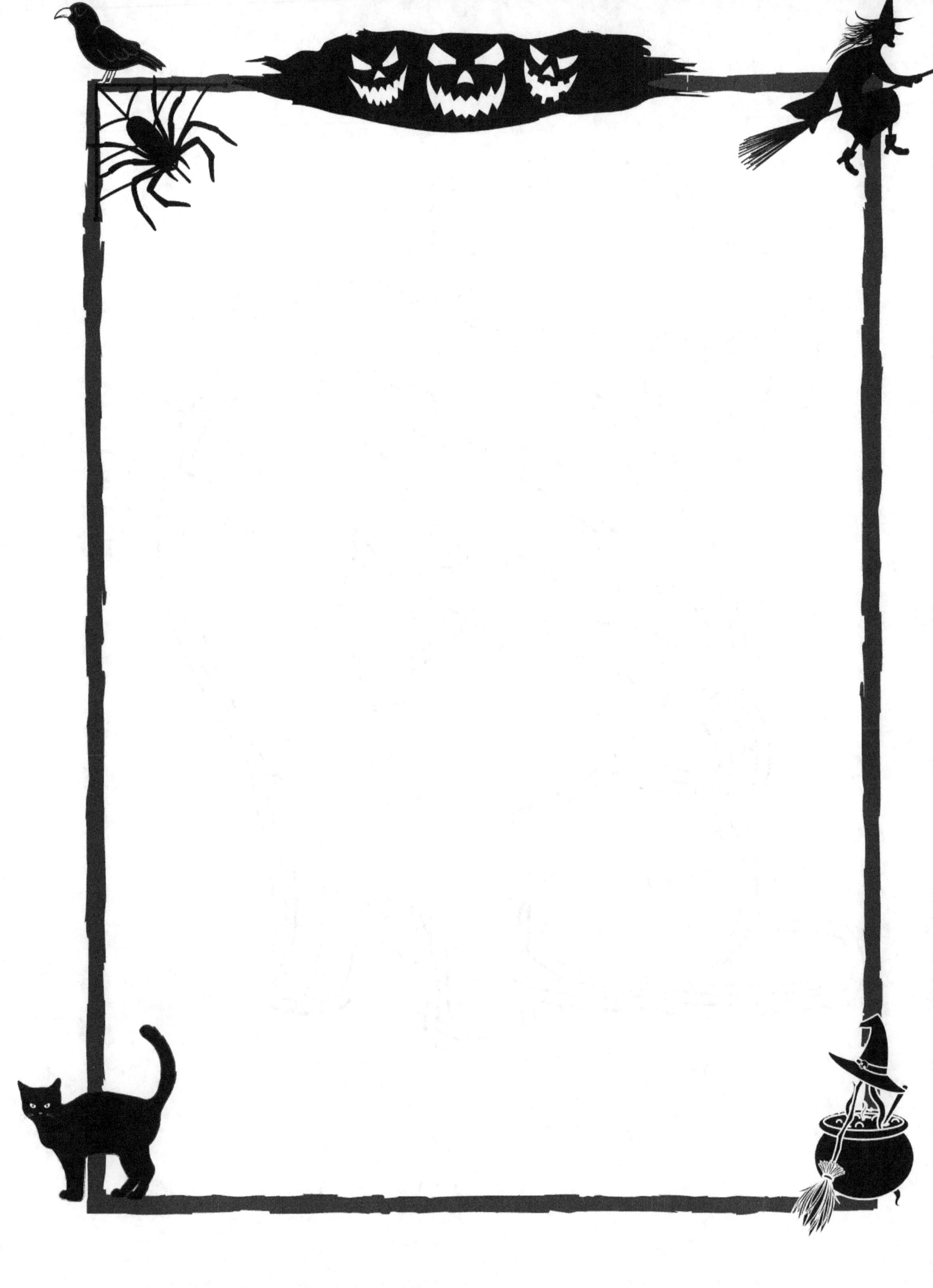

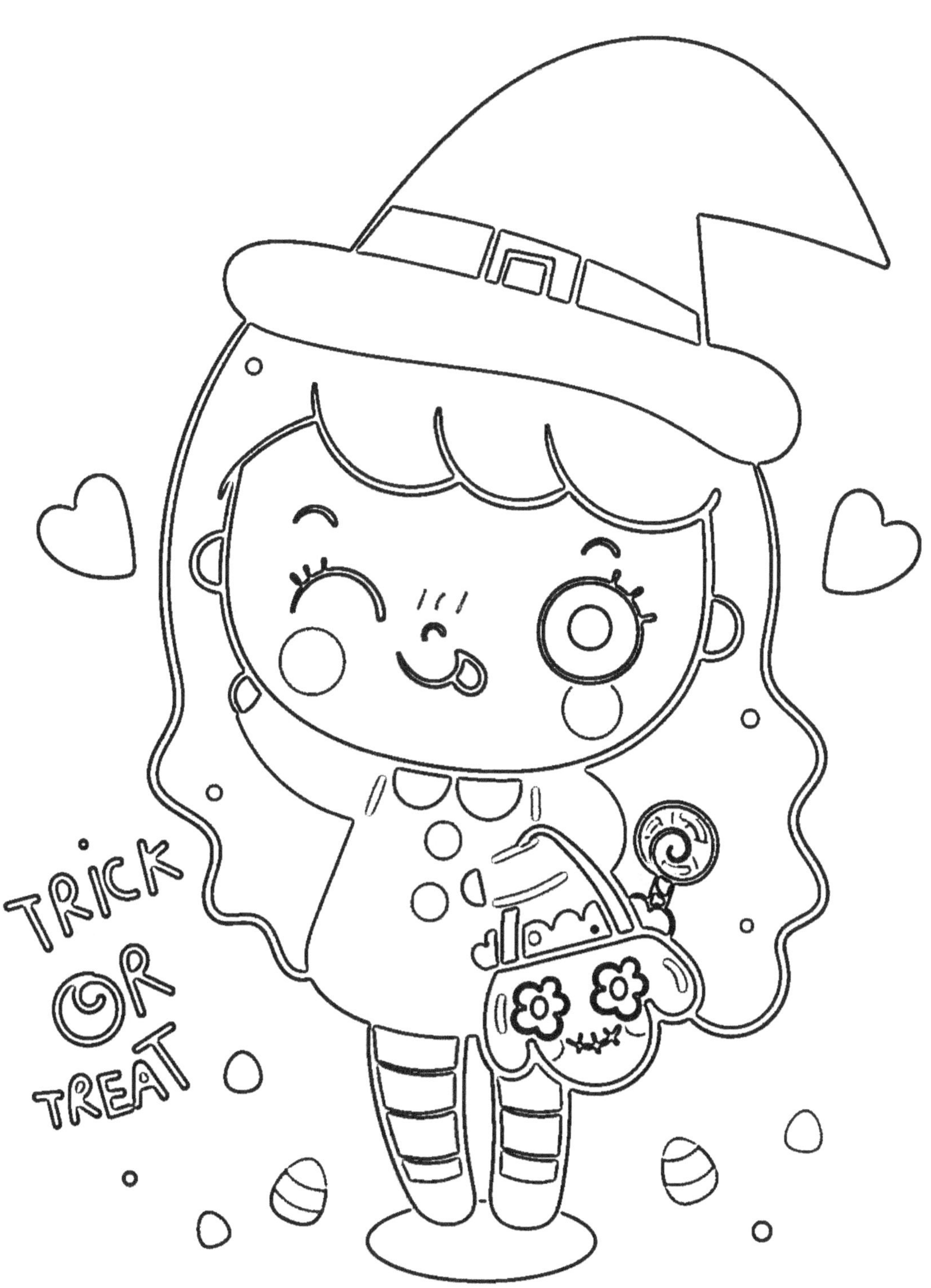
TRICK
OR
TREAT

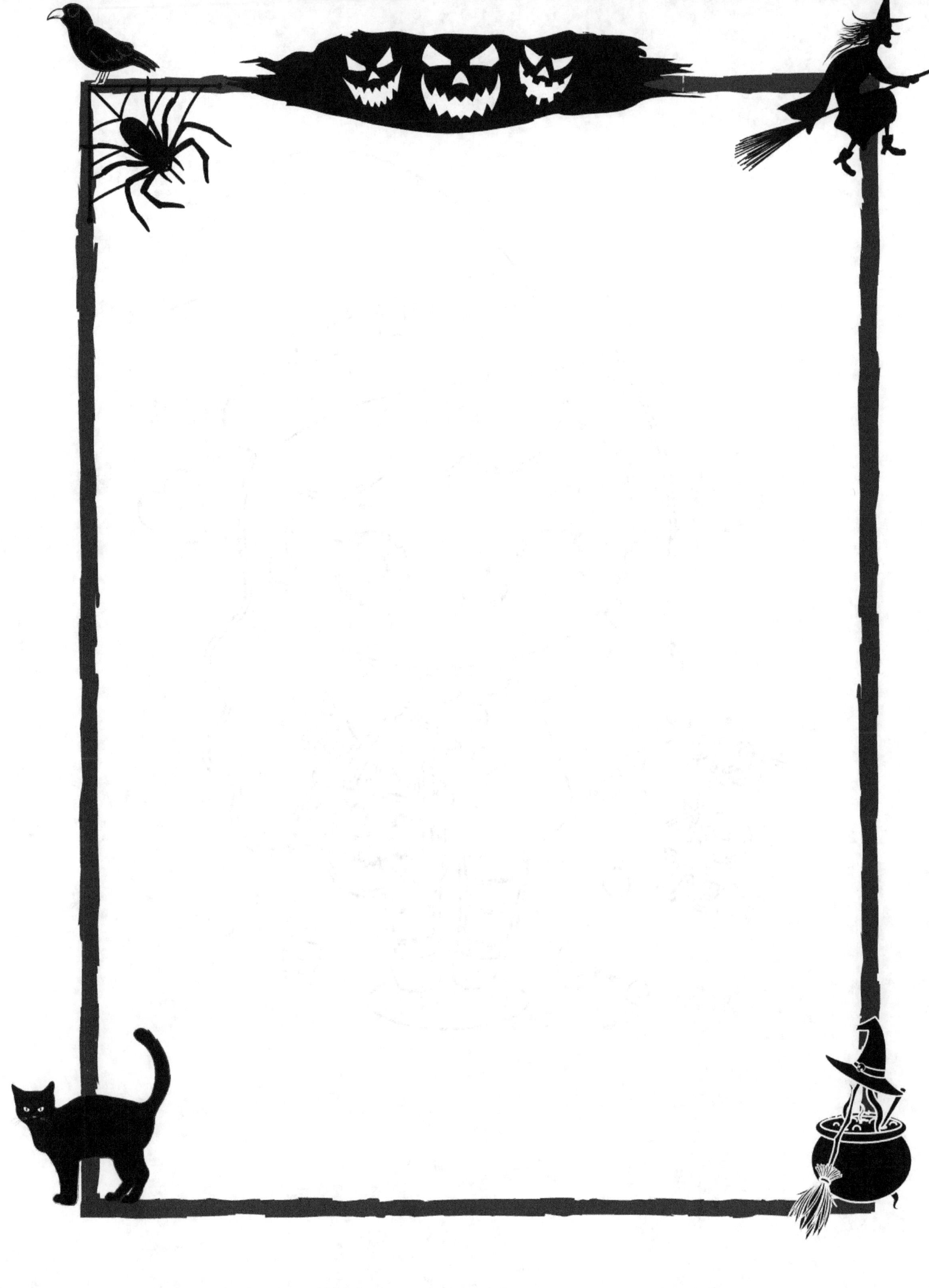

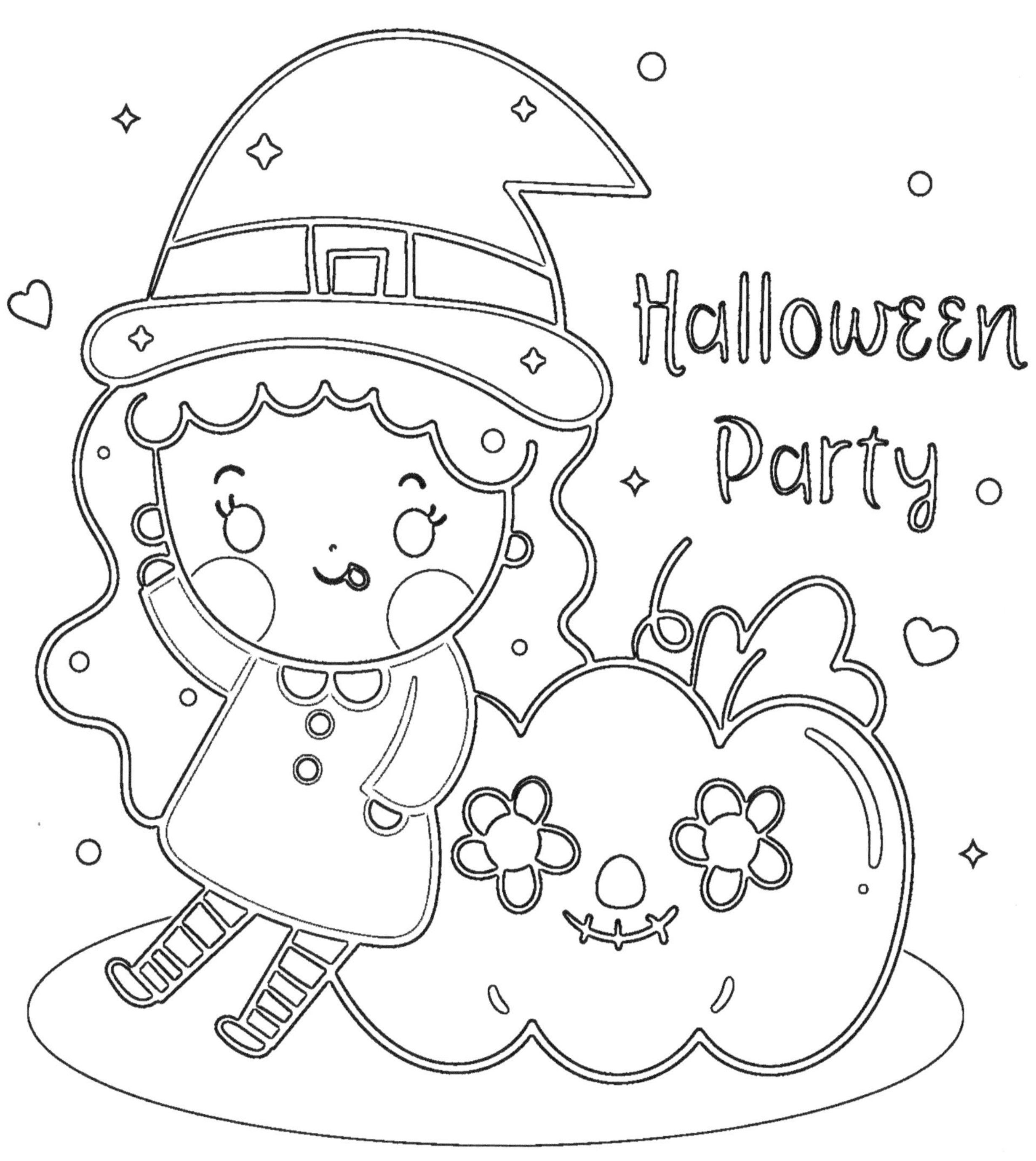

Halloween
Party

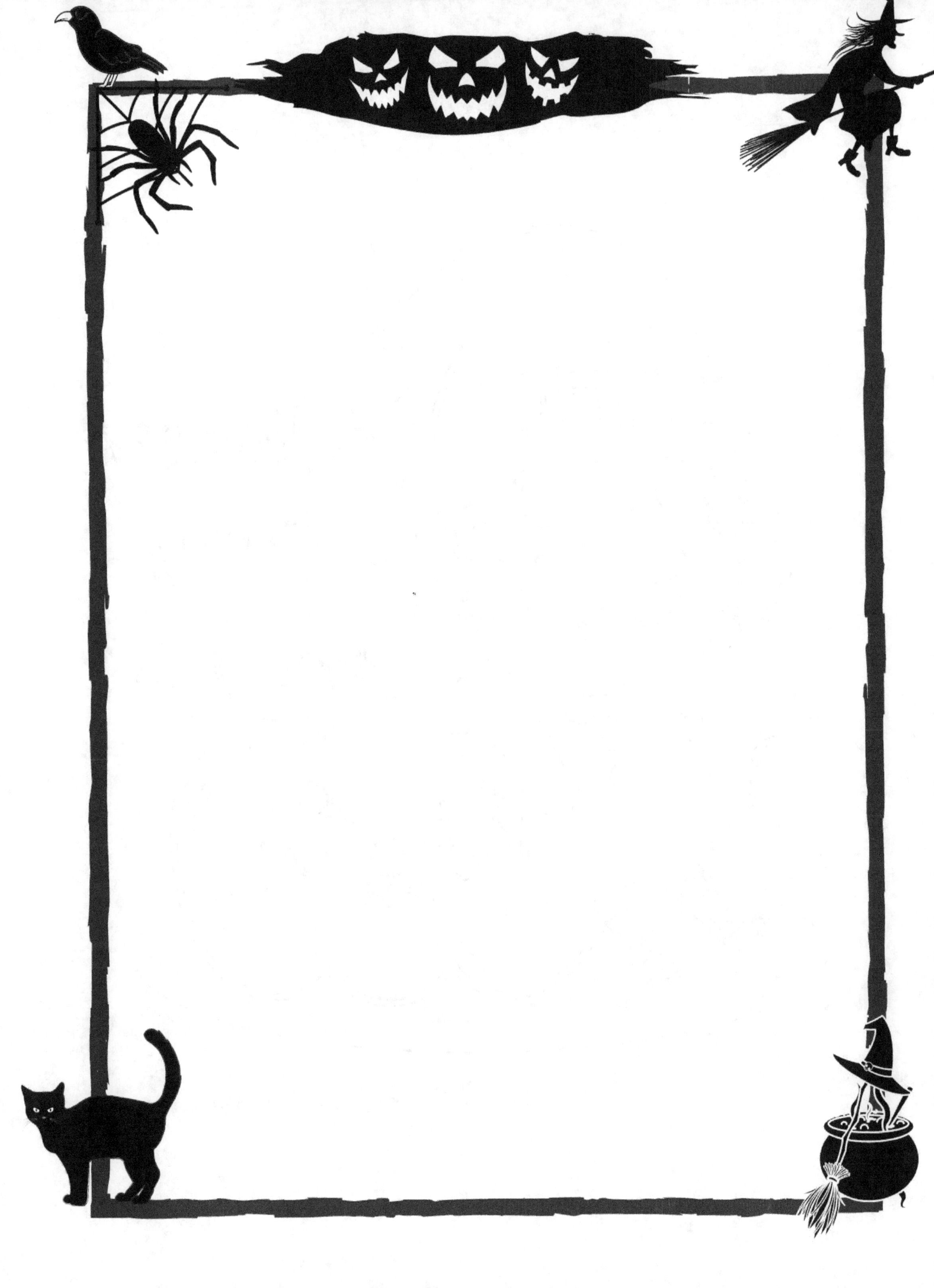

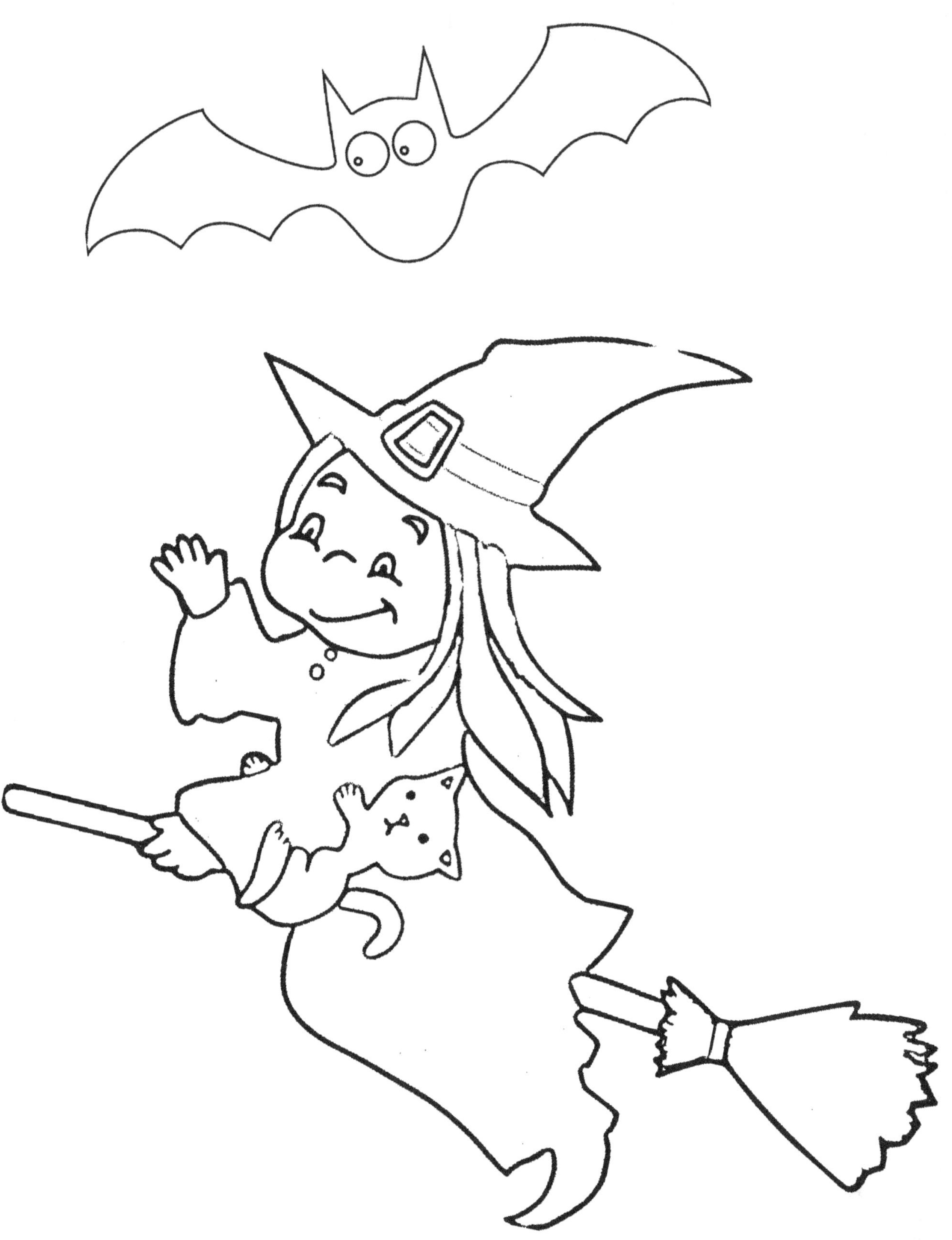

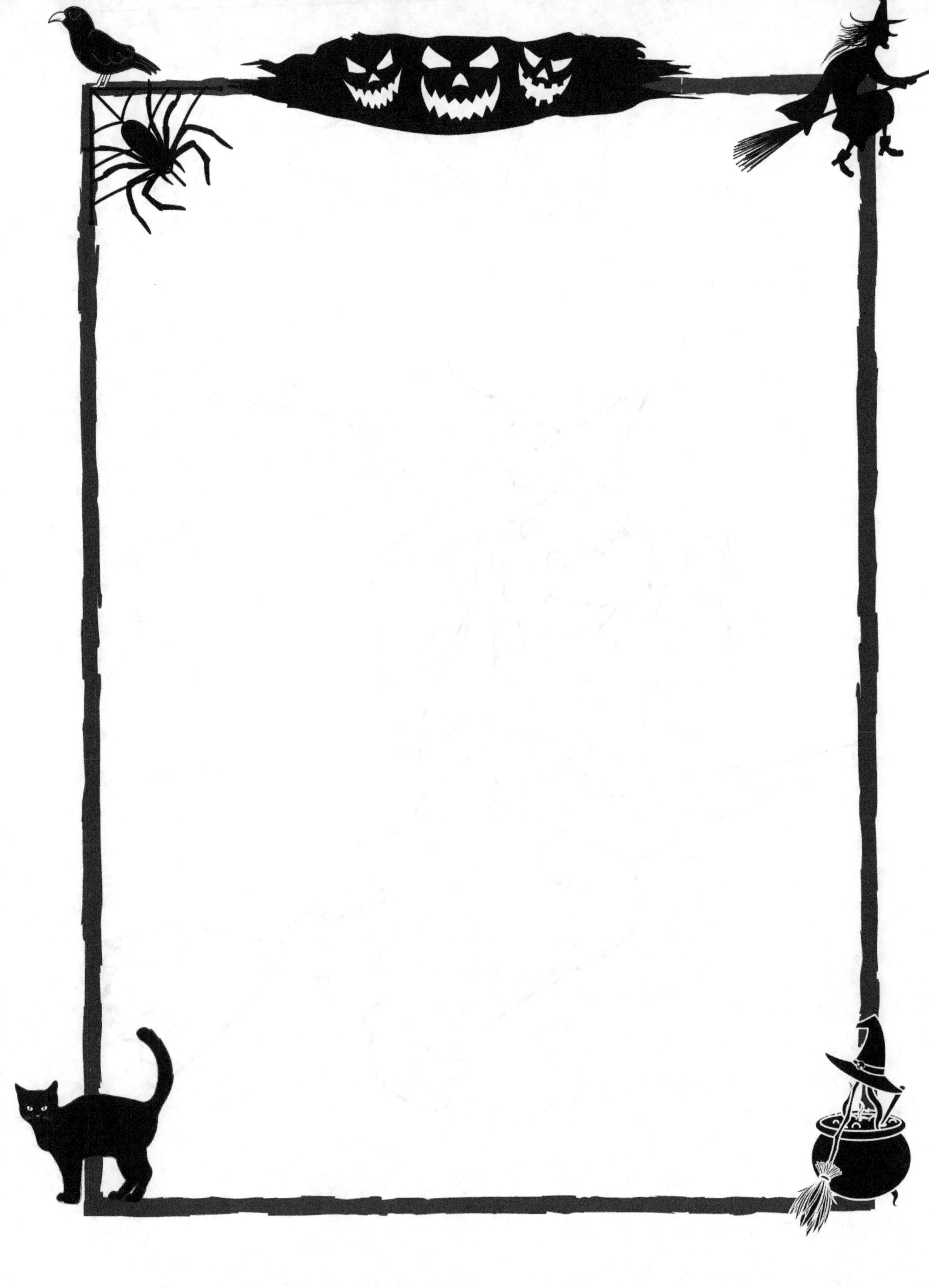

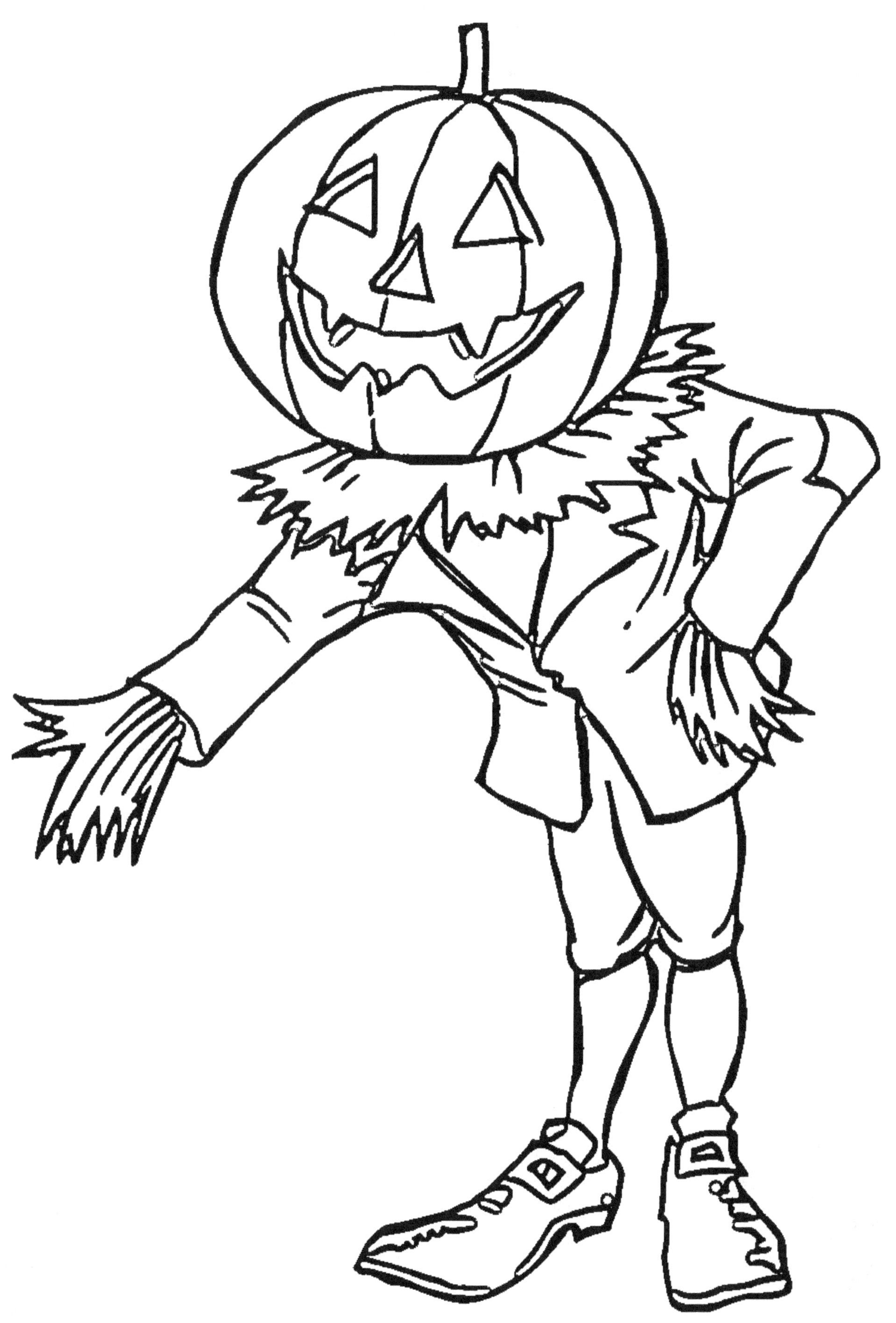

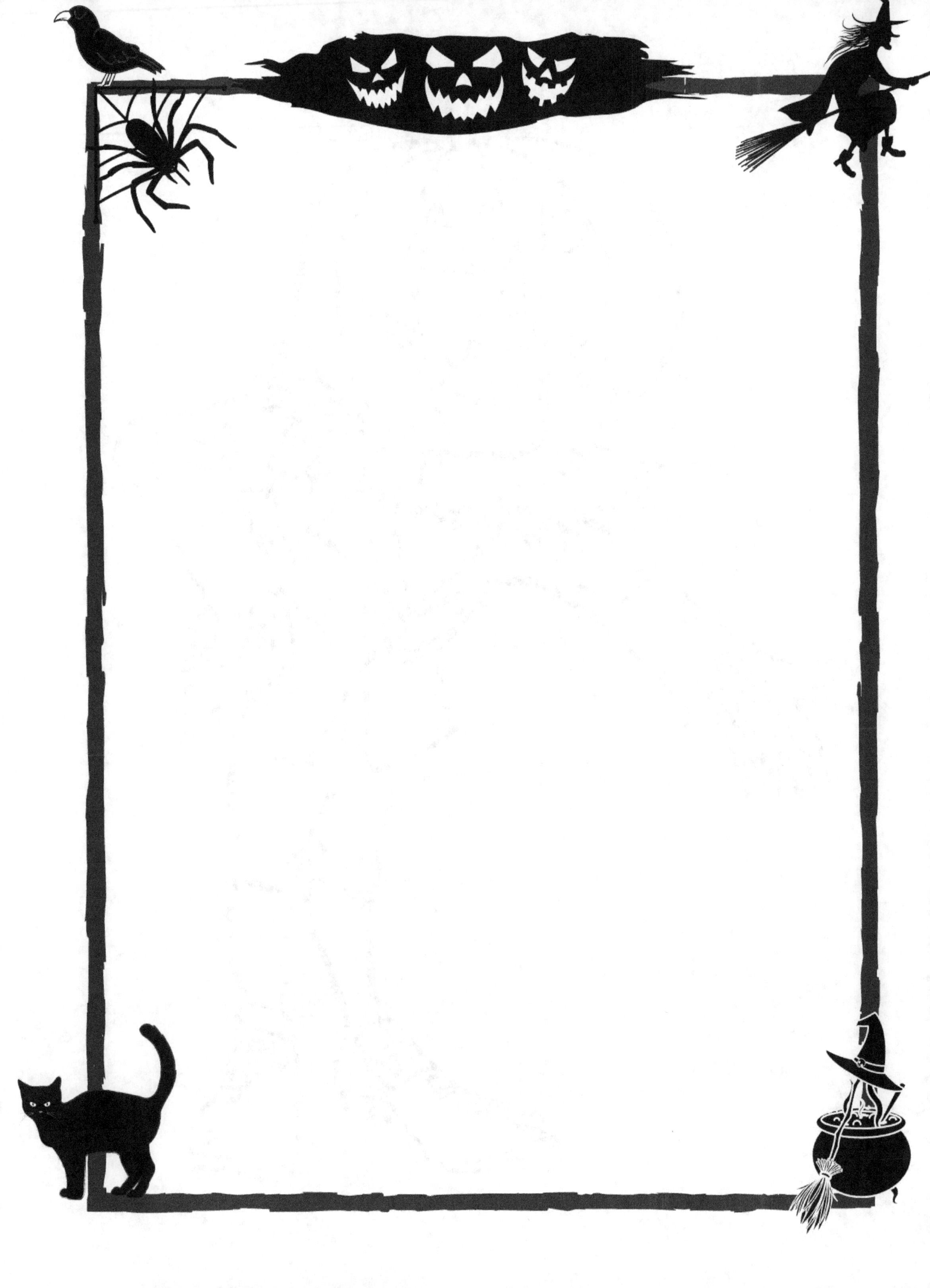

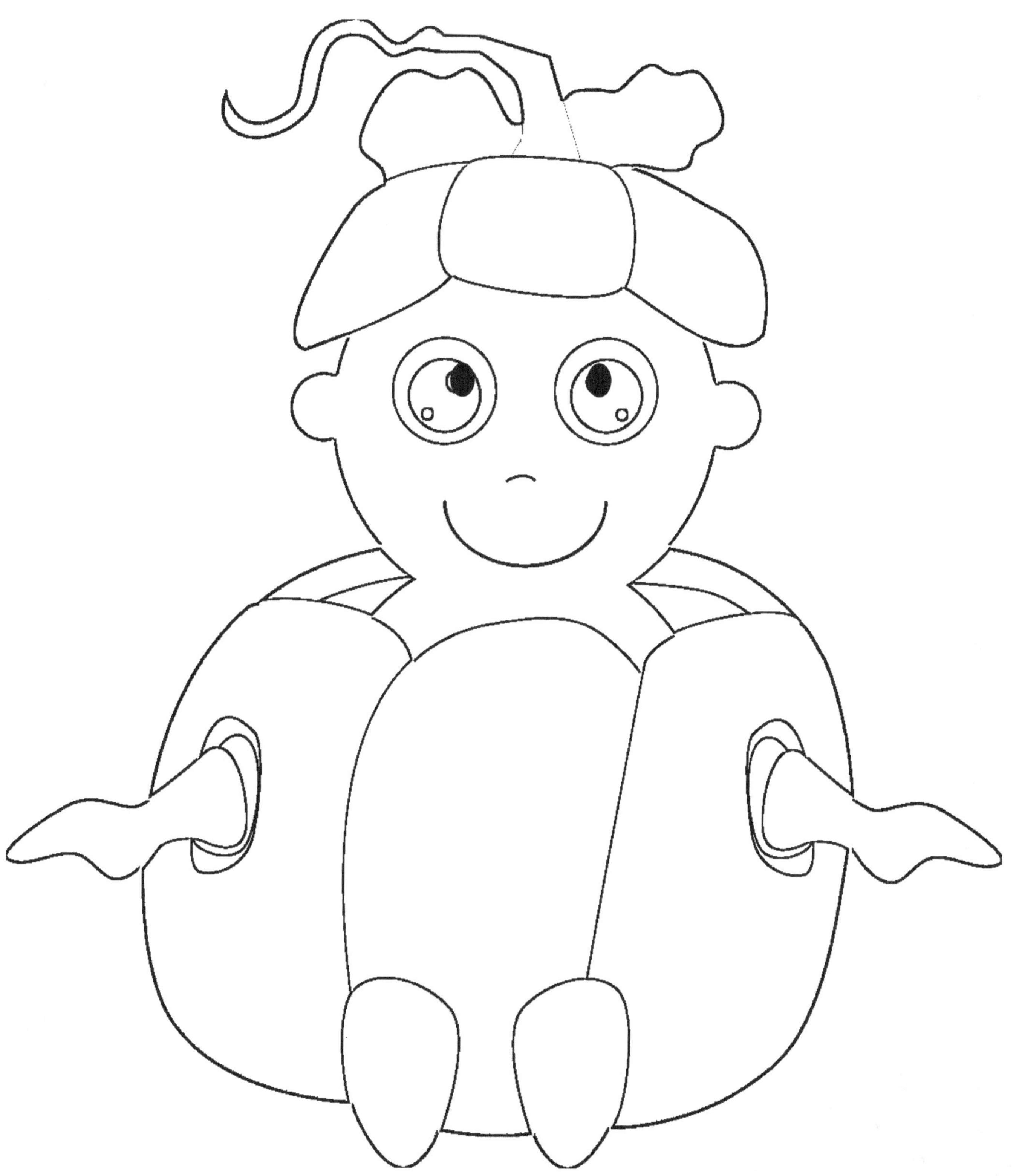

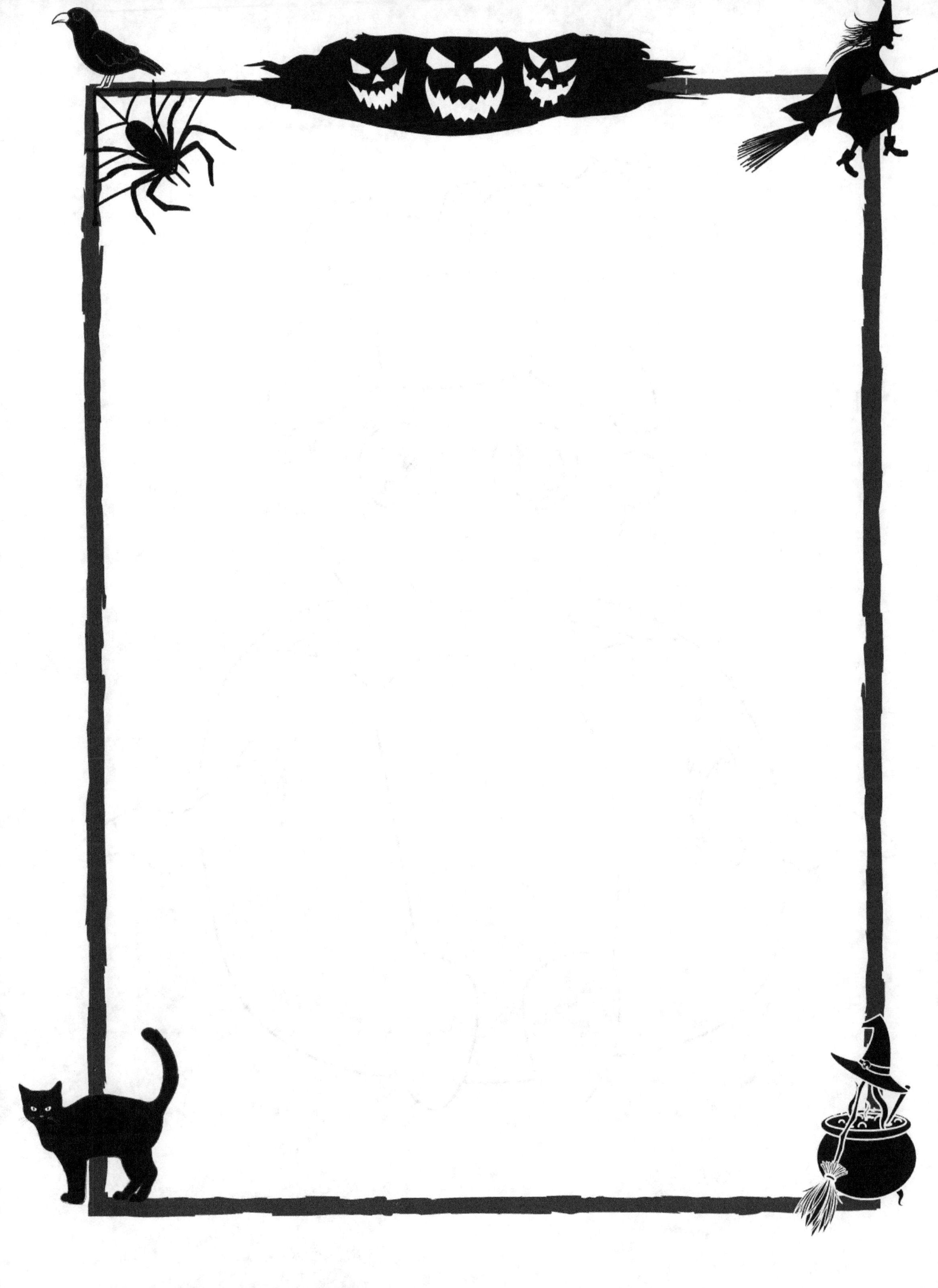

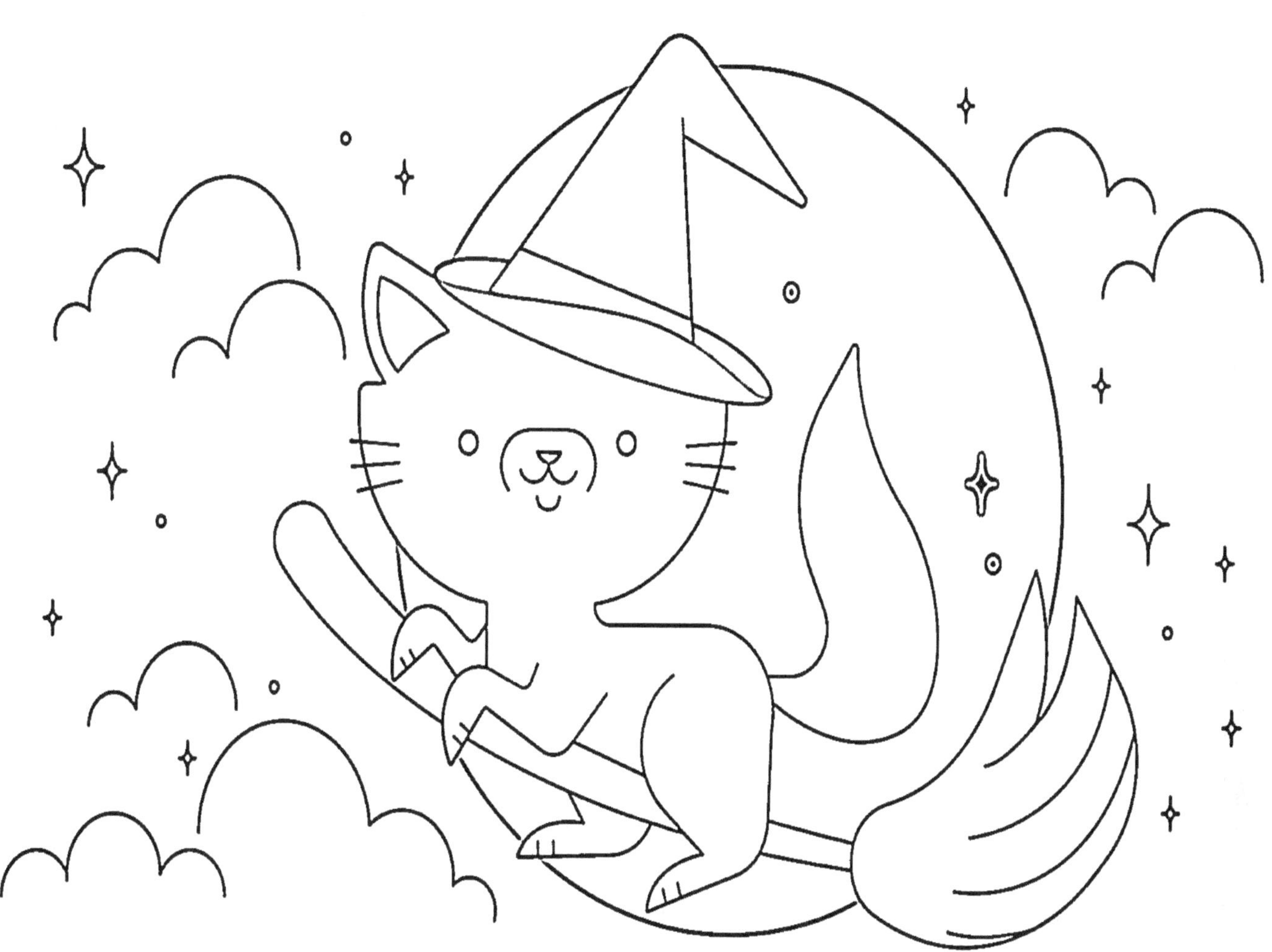

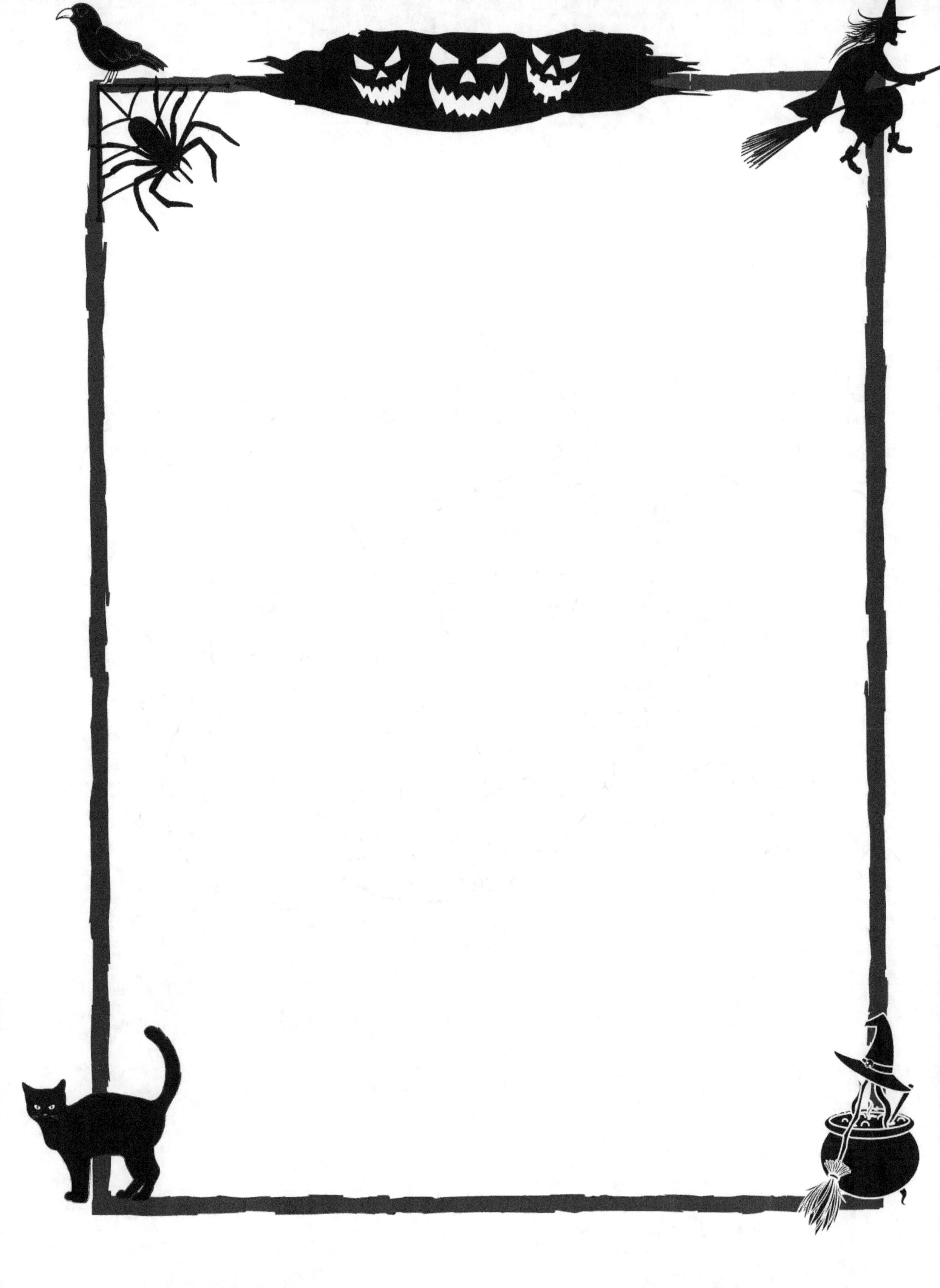

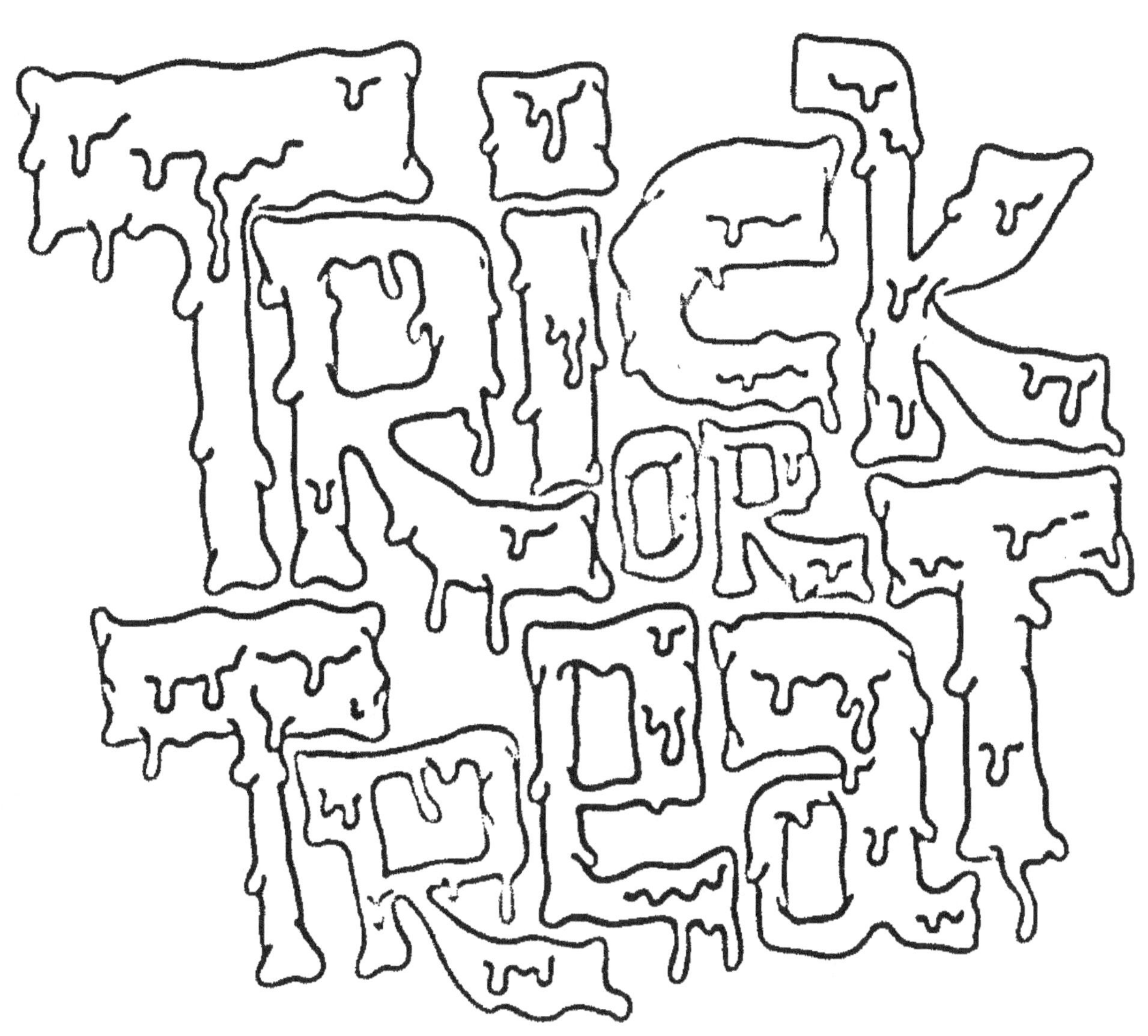

TRICK
OR
TREAT
TREAT

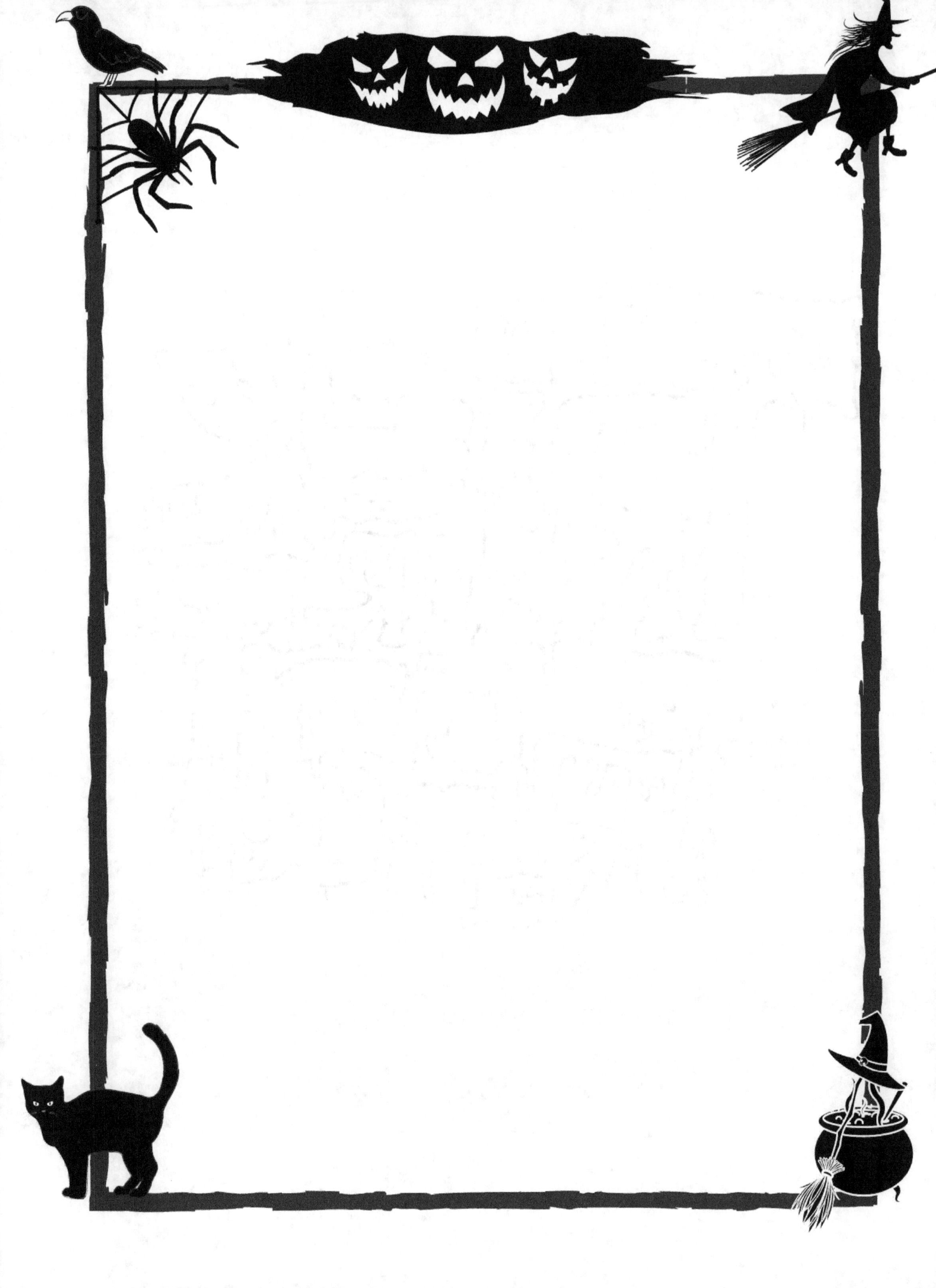

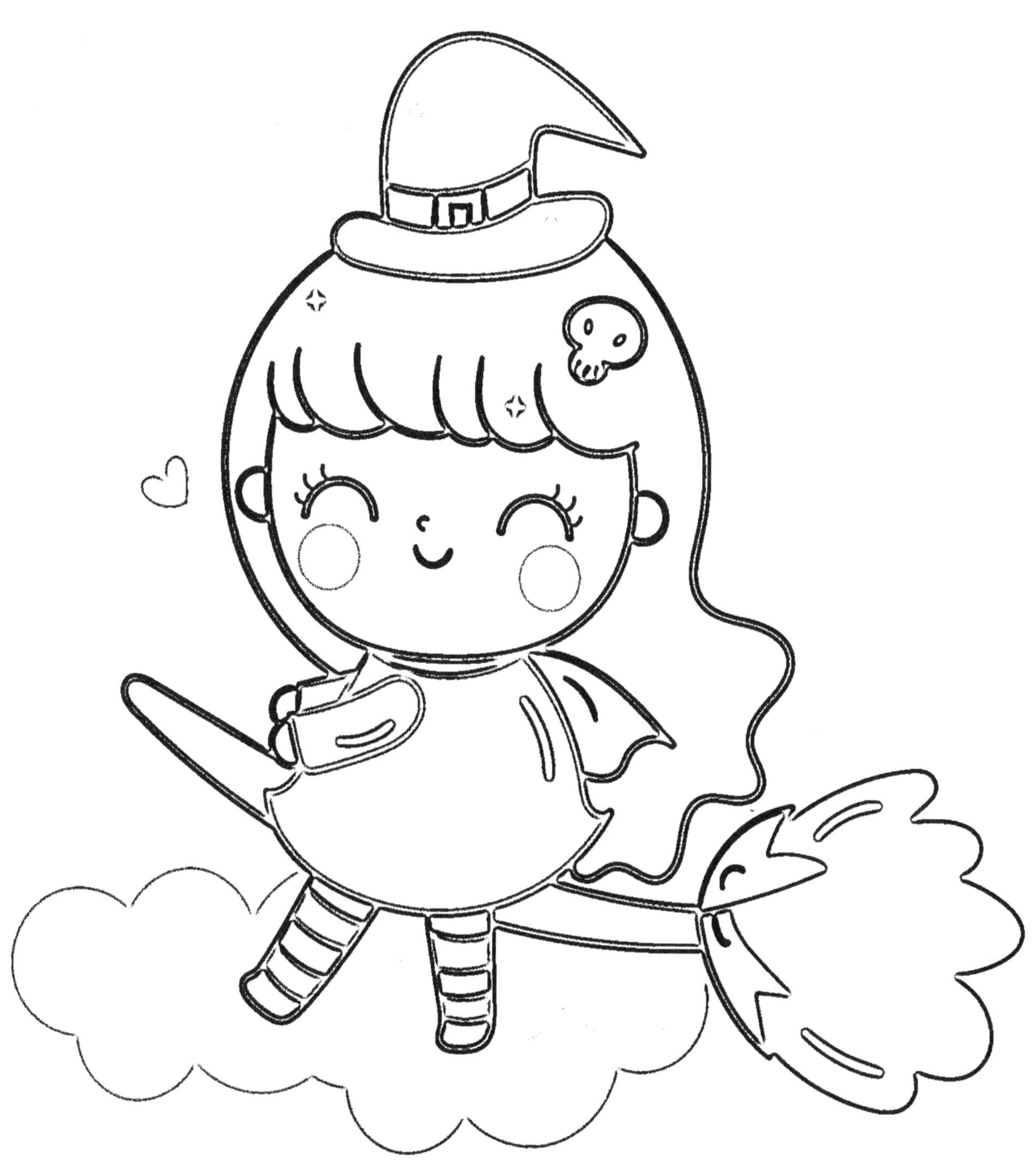

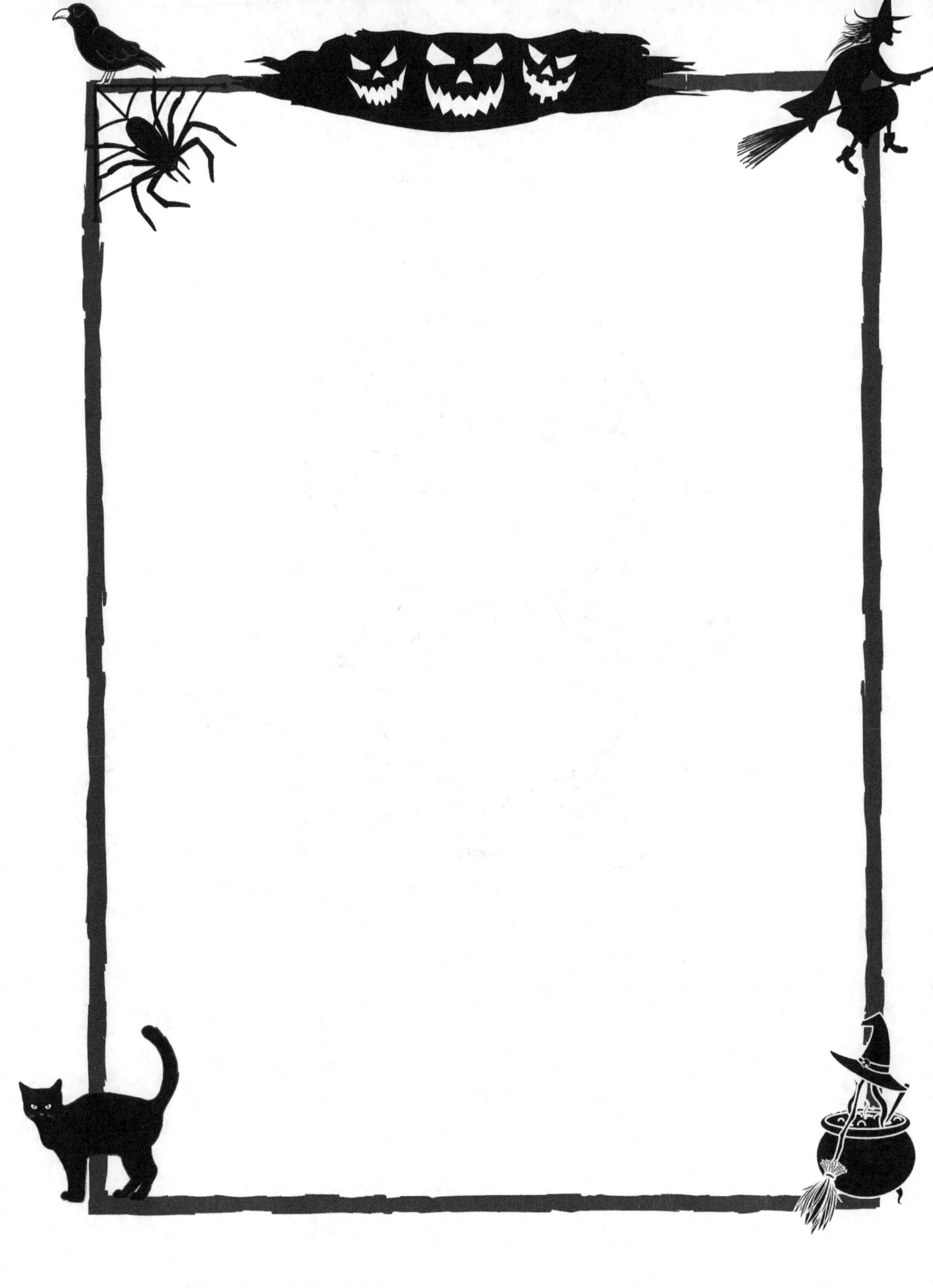

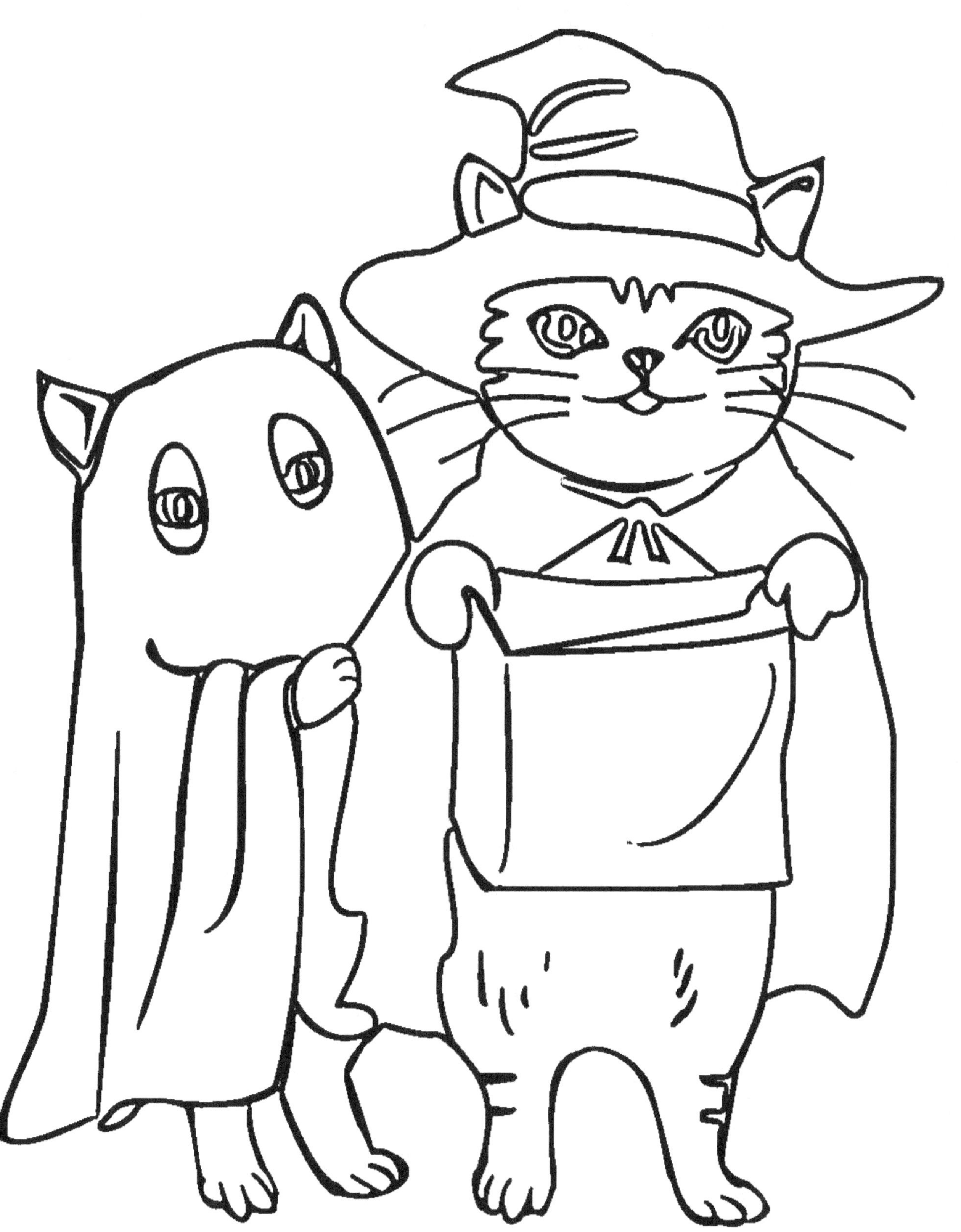

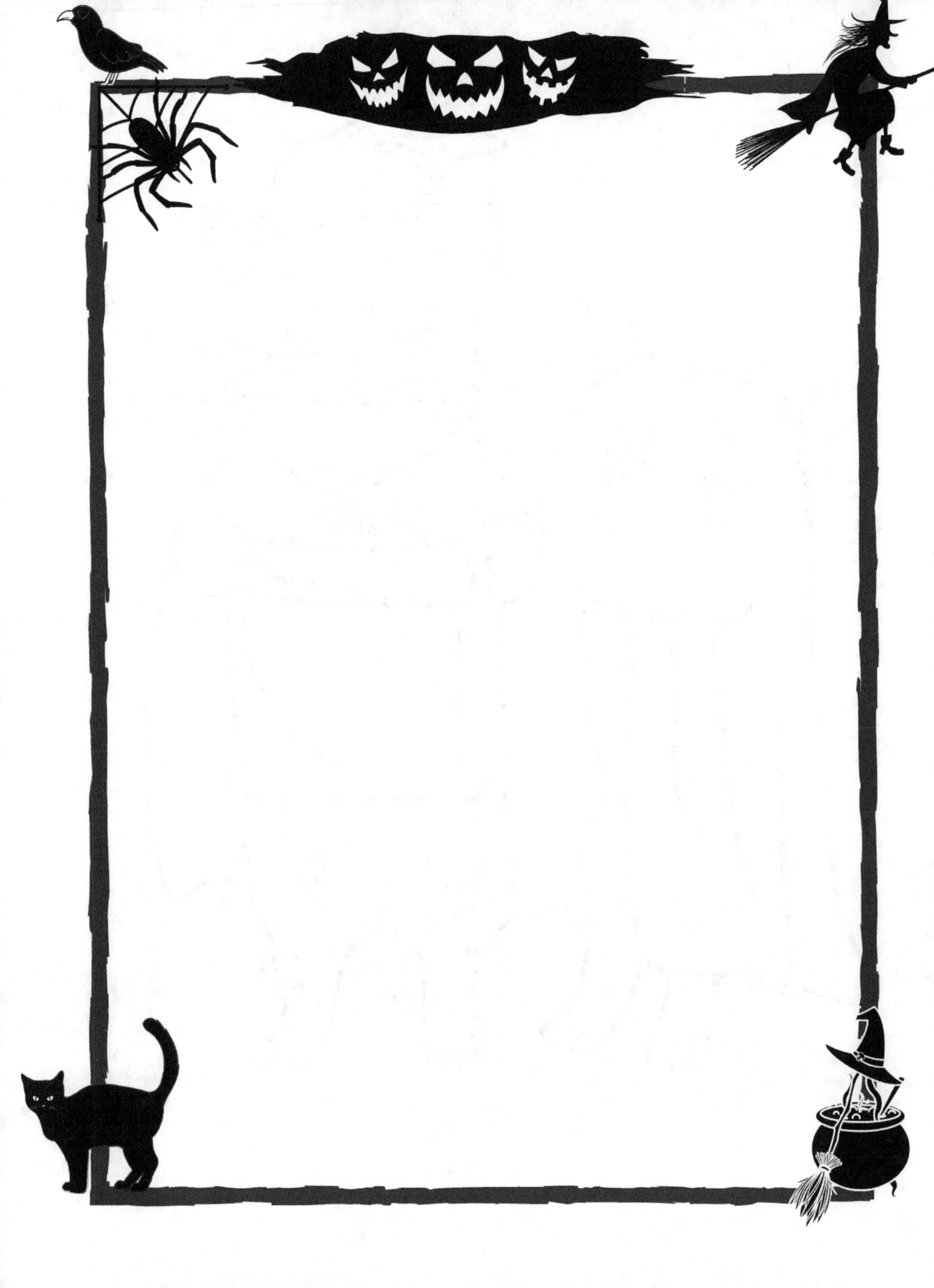